Preserving and Pickling
"Putting Foods By" in Small Batches
By Jacqueline Hériteau and Thalia Erath

Illustrations by Barbara Bascove
Cover photo by Victor Scocozzo

GOLDEN PRESS · NEW YORK
Western Publishing Company, Inc.
Racine, Wisconsin

Foreword

Fruits and vegetables are hardly ever more appealing than when they come right to the table fresh from the garden or local market, at the peak of flavor and ripeness. But because they are seasonal, they can be enjoyed only at certain times of the year. One way of making sure that they are always on your table is to can them; of all the ways of "putting food by," preserving is certainly among the most popular. Preserves confer status on the cook who produces them, draw accolades from family members and proud speeches from spouses, and save quite a lot of money over the cost of fine commercial products. Perhaps best of all, you can take every advantage of ripe fruits and vegetables from your garden, the produce counter, and the gardens of friends who have invariably overextended themselves in their planting.

Preserves are fun to make, and easy. They can be (indeed should be) prepared only in small batches. You can make a few jars in an evening or whenever you have some spare moments, and you need little more equipment than your kitchen probably already has.

Here is a wide-ranging, home-tested collection of recipes for jellies, jams, marmalades, conserves, fruit preserves, butters, relishes, and pickles. Many come from friends, many from our own family files. They will provide you, we trust, with a splendid assortment of unusual and appetite-teasing adornments for your table.

Jacqueline Hériteau
Thalia Erath

Contents

Before You Begin

"Preserves" fall under many names, but basically they are alike in that they are fruits (or vegetables) combined with sugar and usually boiled together.

Jellies are made of clear juice extracted from ripe fruits and boiled with sugar.

Jams are chopped or crushed fruits cooked with sugar to a thick consistency.

Marmalades are made from citrus fruits; the peel, cut thinly, is included.

Conserves are usually made with two or more fruits. Nuts and raisins are often included.

Preserves are whole or cut-up fruits cooked in heavy syrup.

Fruit butters are fruit pulp cooked with sugar and spices to a thick consistency. Butters may be made from the pulp left over from jelly-making if only one extraction of juice was taken.

Relishes are chopped vegetables or fruits cooked with vinegar. Excellent accompaniments to a variety of meats, they can be spicy-hot, or sweet if sugar was added.

Pickles and the art of pickling dealt with in this book call for the quick-process method. The vegetables are covered with salted water to marinate only for a few hours or overnight before being drained and cooked with vinegar, sugar, and spices.

In making these recipes, you run no risk of botulism or of bacteria that can cause spoilage because you will be using natural food preservatives. Sugar, salt, and vinegar are time-proven preservatives that naturally inhibit the growth of harmful bacteria.

EQUIPMENT

The equipment needed for making the recipes in this book is available in most home kitchens. To make jelly or jam, you'll need:

☐ A large kettle for sterilizing glasses and jars, cooking the fruit, and for processing by the Boiling-Water Bath method (page 9)

☐ A broad, shallow kettle for cooking juice and sugar, and for making relishes

☐ A measuring cup

☐ A long-handled spoon

☐ A ladle

☐ Cheesecloth to use as a jelly bag for straining fruit juice

☐ A metal strainer or colander to hold the cheesecloth

☐ A large bowl to catch the juice as it drains

☐ Jelly glasses with lids, and/or canning jars

☐ Labels

Use only glass, enameled, or heat-resistant plastic equipment; metal in contact with the acid in fruit can cause discoloration.

As your skill increases, you may want to add other pieces of equipment such as funnels of various sizes, a jelly thermometer, a food mill, a jelly bag, and perhaps a kitchen scale.

ABOUT CONTAINERS

Some preserves require processing by heating in a boiling-water bath. Many preserves that cook for a very long time may not need to be processed; this depends primarily on your storage conditions. Preserves which will be processed must be turned into regular canning jars with lids (page 7). Jellies, and preserves that are not processed, can be packed into "found" containers and jelly glasses, and sealed with paraffin (page 8).

CANNING JARS

Canning jars, made of tempered glass to withstand high temperatures, are sold in a variety of sizes; in this book we recommend the use of half- or one-pint jars. Some jars are wide-mouthed with straight sides, others have shoulders. Lids and ring bands are included when you buy new canning jars. The ring bands can be used repeatedly if they are in good condition, but the metal lids must be replaced each time as the sealing compound is effective only once.

If the jars are the type requiring separate rubber rings, test the rings before using, even if they are brand new. Fold them into small pleats; if they crack, discard them. Or stretch them: if they don't return to the original shape, they are useless.

1. This jar, the vacuum type, is the kind most commonly used for jellies, and for jams which are not processed in the Boiling-Water Bath. To seal when processing, place the flat metal lid on the filled jar, the sealing compound side next to the glass. Holding the lid down, screw the band on firmly, then process as directed. After processing, remove jars from the kettle and let cool on a towel away from drafts.

2. Canning jars with porcelain-lined zinc caps are hard to come by today—your grandmother's attic may be the best place to look for them! To use, fit a moistened rubber ring down on the shoulder of an empty jar. Pack the jar, wipe off the rubber ring and jar rim, screw the zinc cap down firmly, then turn it back ¼ inch. After processing, remove the jar from the kettle and immediately screw the cap down tightly to complete the seal.

3. To use jars with glass lids, moisten the rubber ring and place it on the lid. Place the lid on the jar with the rubber ring against the rim. Put on the screw band, screw it down tightly, then turn it back ¼ inch. After processing, remove the jar from the kettle and immediately screw the band down tightly to complete the seal.

4. The glass lids on these old-fashioned "lightening jars" are held down by a wire bail. Fit the moistened rubber ring to the little "ledge" at the top of the jar. Press the glass lid on the ring. Pull the longer wire clamp up and over the top of the glass lid, fitting it into the groove on the lid. Leave the smaller wire up while processing, then immediately snap it down to seal the jar as you remove it from the kettle. Note: Heat-proof "gift shop" lightening jars of untempered glass are fine for unprocessed preserves, but do not subject them to high temperatures.

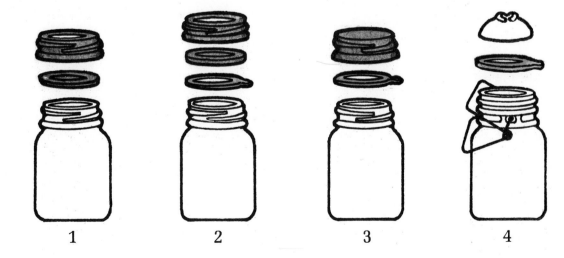

1   2   3   4

STERILIZING GLASSES AND JARS

We do not sterilize jars and glasses. Years ago our favorite pediatrician told us that washing dishes in a dishwasher provided all the sterilizing that was needed, even when children had contagious diseases. To us, then, this method seems safe enough for preserve containers. However, if you wish to sterilize jars and glasses—and you might want to sterilize some "found" containers—then wash the containers and their lids, if any, in soapy water, rinse thoroughly, and boil gently in water to cover for 15 to 20 minutes.

Canning jars for relishes, pickles, and preserves that are to be subjected to processing should be washed thoroughly in hot, soapy water, rinsed well, and air-dried. These jars are not likely to benefit from sterilizing, since the processing takes place in boiling water and will kill any harmful bacteria.

SEALING METHODS

When the recipes in this book instruct you to seal jellies or unprocessed preserves, you should cover the contents of the glass or jar with melted paraffin, as described below.

When the word "seal" is used in connection with containers that will be subjected to the Boiling-Water Bath (page 9), it means to place the lids on the canning jars. The four types of canning jars for processing are illustrated on page 7. Instructions accompany each illustration. In each case, the lid is placed on the jar before processing begins. Processing completes, or helps complete, the sealing, according to jar type.

The paraffin seal is the one most often used to seal jellies and jams in "found" containers and jelly glasses. Here's how it's done:

1. Melt paraffin over hot water. Note: Do not melt paraffin directly over the flame or burner; it catches fire easily. Transfer the melted paraffin to a pitcher or teapot, then carefully pour a thin layer over the contents in the glasses. Swirl the hot paraffin around until it covers the edges of the glasses just above the jelly. The paraffin should be about 1/8 inch thick. Allow the glasses to cool, pricking any air bubbles that appear on the wax surface (these could prevent a tight seal).

2. When the wax is hard, cut circles or squares of plastic wrap a little larger than the tops of the jelly glasses. Cover the glasses with the plastic, pulling it tightly and smoothly over the tops.

3. Cover the glasses with lids, if you have them, or use a piece of foil, fastened tightly with string or tape.

Jelly glasses that are sold with so-called vacuum-pack lids do not require a paraffin seal, as a rule. Sealing instructions are included with the manufacturer's directions. The vacuum produced between the lid and the contents in this type of container is not the same kind of vacuum seal that is a result of processing. In other words, don't expect that packing hot preserves into this type of glass and sealing it will replace the processing phase.

Once in a while, it happens that you run out of paraffin in the middle of sealing a batch of preserves. If so, seal by stretching plastic wrap or plain white paper over the top of the glass and tie it in place with string. Such tops rip easily, however, and aren't the best way to seal jellies and jams that are to be stored for a long period of time.

BOILING-WATER BATH PROCESSING

If your storage conditions are far less than ideal—for instance, a too-warm, centrally heated home or apartment or a warm, humid climate—it is a good idea to build into your preserves extra protection from mold or other spoilage by treating all jams, marmalades, conserves, relishes, butters, and pickles with a short Boiling-Water Bath before storing. Note: Jelly is the only exception. Do not process jelly in a Boiling-Water Bath.

Preserves processed in a Boiling-Water Bath must be put up in canning jars and are not sealed with paraffin. For a discussion of the different kinds of canning jars, see page 7.

To process in a Boiling-Water Bath:

1. Have ready a very deep kettle or canning kettle filled with hot (not boiling) water. The kettle must be deep enough to ensure that the tops of the jars will be covered by 2 inches of boiling water.

2. When the preserves have cooked, fill the hot jars to within ½ inch of the tops (or as recipe directs). Wipe off the jar rims. Place the lids on the jars as illustrated on page 7.

3. Place the jars on a rack in the kettle and pour in enough rapidly boiling water to cover the jars by 2 inches. Do not pour the water directly on the jars. Cover the kettle with a close-fitting lid and, over high heat, bring the water back to the boiling point.

4. Start to count the time required for processing when the water returns to a boil; boil steadily for the number of minutes that the recipe indicates.

5. Remove the jars immediately and complete seals if necessary. Let cool on a wire rack away from drafts.

6. To test jars to make sure that they are vacuum-sealed, press down on the center of the lid after cooling; if it stays down, the jar is sealed. If you're unsure about the seal, tilt the jar; if any liquid seeps through, the seal is not perfect and you must reprocess the contents, use them immediately, or freeze the preserves in the imperfectly sealed jars. (Imperfect seals are frequently the result of food remaining on the jar rims before sealing.)

Note: Processing times given in this book are for altitudes less than 1,000 feet above sea level. For altitudes above 1,000 feet, use this chart. If a recipe calls for more than 20 minutes of processing time, the increased times given in this chart should be doubled.

Altitude (Feet)	Increase in Processing Time (Minutes)
Above 1,000	1
Above 2,000	2
Above 3,000	3
Above 4,000	4
Above 5,000	5
Above 6,000	6
Above 7,000	7
Above 8,000	8
Above 9,000	9
Above 10,000	10

SUGAR SUBSTITUTES

With recurrent sugar shortages and consequent high prices, you may want to consider a sugar substitute such as honey or corn syrup. Many of these substitutes, however, are often more expensive than sugar. (We prefer to use granulated sugar; in penny-pinching moments, we make fewer jars.) There will be a difference in flavor when a sugar substitute is used. Corn syrup is about half as sweet as granulated sugar; preserves sweetened with it are less sweet than those made with sugar. Light corn syrup is the best sugar substitute in jellies. Use dark corn syrup in chutneys, butters, relishes, and pickles, where appearance is not as important.

To prepare preserves with honey or corn syrup, follow the recipe, but use half the amount of granulated sugar called for and use honey or corn syrup for the other half. Note that jellies made with honey or corn syrup take longer to reach the jelly stage (page 14); also, they cause the juice to foam up to a greater volume while cooking, so you will need a bigger kettle. We recommend that preserves with sugar substitutes be processed in a Boiling-Water Bath for 10 minutes.

Brown sugar is fine as a substitute for white sugar in butters or conserves, but is not good for jellies. Substitute an equal amount of brown sugar for granulated white, but make sure it is very firmly packed into the measuring cup.

Maple sugar adds its own flavor and is scarce and expensive. Don't use it in jellies. Use half the amount of granulated sugar called for and use maple sugar for the remainder.

Molasses, like brown sugar, has its own strong flavor. We do not consider it a good substitute for granulated sugar in these recipes.

SPICES

Many recipes for relishes call for spices such as ginger, cinnamon, cloves, allspice, and nutmeg. When possible, use whole spices: stick cinnamon or its relative, cassia buds; whole allspice berries; whole cloves or nutmeg. Tie them in a piece of clean cloth or cheesecloth for easy removal after cooking.

If you do use ground or powdered spices, use the freshest products possible. If you have kept spices on your kitchen shelf longer than six months, throw them away and get a fresh supply—we mean it! Old spices don't do the job.

Gingerroot is the rhizome of a tropical plant, *Zingiber officinale*, grown in the East and West Indies, Africa, and China. Jamaican ginger, sold in Chinese food shops and many fruit markets, is considered the best. If you find a fresh, shiny-skinned piece of root, plant it just below soil level in a pot filled with indoor-plant potting soil. Place it in a sunny window, water it, and let it grow until the roots fill the pot. Then cut off a piece to root in another pot—and use your ginger fresh or frozen for cooking, preserving, and pickling. To use grated fresh gingerroot, use a fine grater such as a nutmeg grater. One teaspoon grated fresh ginger equals ½ teaspoon ground dried ginger.

Jellies

Jellies

Jelly is simply clear, strained fruit juice cooked with sugar until thickened. Good jelly is clear, sparkling, and gemlike in its translucency. The finished product quivers yet holds its shape. It is not syrupy, gummy, tough, or rubbery. It spreads easily, and the flavor is fresh and fruity.

Essential ingredients in jelly are fresh fruits, for their individual flavors; pectin (found naturally in many fruits) which, in combination with the acid of the fruit, causes the juice to jell; and sugar, a preserving aid that helps the gel to form and adds flavor to the finished product. (If you wish to use sweeteners other than sugar, refer to page 10.)

FRUITS RICH IN PECTIN AND ACID

Tart apples
Blackberries
Crab apples
Cranberries
Currants
Gooseberries
Grapes
Loganberries
Beach plums (use slightly underripe fruit)
Raspberries (use slightly underripe fruit)

FRUITS RICH IN PECTIN, LOW IN ACID

To increase the acid content of these fruits sufficiently, add ½ to 1 tablespoon lemon juice per cup of fruit juice.
Sweet apples
Citron melons
Figs
Oranges
Pears
Quinces

FRUITS RICH IN ACID, LOW IN PECTIN

Combine these fruits with other fruits that are rich in pectin or use commercial pectin.
Apricots
Sour cherries
Pineapples
Pomegranates
Rhubarb (vegetable)
Strawberries

FRUITS LOW IN ACID AND PECTIN

Juices from these fruits can be made into jelly by using commercial pectin.
Elderberries
Peaches
Pears
Raspberries (when ripe)

COMMERCIAL PECTIN

Commercially prepared pectin is processed from natural fruits, usually apples, and marketed in powdered and liquid forms. There are advantages in using commercial pectin: There is no guesswork or waste, and the short cooking period saves time, insures good flavor and color, and increases the yield by as much as one-third to one-half. Follow directions exactly when using commercial pectin. The major disadvantage in using commercial pectin is that large amounts of sugar are needed; thus, the jellies are often too sweet.

JELLY GLASSES

For quivering, shimmering cylinders of jelly, use the straight-sided six- or eight-ounce jelly glasses which allow for easy unmolding. But if you have glasses of other shapes on hand, by all means use them. Just be sure that they are not cracked and that there are no nicks on the rims.
It is not necessary to sterilize jelly glasses before use. A thorough wash in hot, soapy water and a thorough rinse in hot water (or a wash in a dishwasher) are enough.

MAKING JELLY: GENERAL DIRECTIONS

1. Choose a clear, dry day for making jelly; a damp, humid day actually adds moisture to the cooking pot and slows down the jelling process. Work in mini-batches — they are easier to handle and take less time than larger quantities.

2. Wash fruit, remove stems, and cut out any bad spots. Add water according to juiciness of fruit. Cook, covered, just long enough to extract the juice — overcooking breaks down the pectin. Soft fruits will require 5 to 10 minutes of cooking; hard fruits, 15 to 30 minutes. Crush soft berries slightly before cooking to start the juices flowing.

3. Strain the juice through a dampened jelly bag or wet doubled cheesecloth; twist the bag and press out the juice. When you are working with fruits rich in acid and pectin, a second extraction may be made. Return the pulp to the kettle, barely cover with water, simmer 30 minutes, then strain. Combine the two extractions.

4. Measure the juice and boil, uncovered, 5 minutes; then add the sugar. Return to a full rolling boil and boil rapidly, uncovered, until the jelly (or "sheeting") stage, described on the following page, is reached. If you are using a jelly thermometer, the jelly stage is 220 to 222° F.

5. Remove from heat, skim the foam, and pour the syrup into hot, clean, dry jelly glasses to within ½ inch of the tops. Don't leave any syrup on the inside rim of the glass; clean it carefully, so that the hot paraffin will seal tightly. Seal with hot paraffin and plastic wrap (page 8).

6. When the glasses are cool, put on the lids. Label the jellies and store in a cool, dark place.

THE JELLY TEST

The jelly, or "sheeting," stage is the point at which the juice and sugar have cooked enough to jell. This is reached when a jelly thermometer registers 220 to 222° F. However, double-check for best results, using the jelly test as well as the thermometer.

To test, take a cold metal spoon and dip up some of the boiling syrup. Pour it off the

spoon, back into the pot. When the last two drops on the spoon cling together to form a sheet and drop off very slowly, or if they cling to the edge of the spoon, the jelly, or "sheeting," stage has been reached.

Another test is to dip a silver fork into the syrup. When the syrup sheets over the tines, the jelly stage has been reached.

WHEN YOUR JELLY ISN'T PERFECT

Here are some of the causes of failure in jelly-making:

Too soft: too much sugar was added.

Tough and rubbery: not enough sugar was added, or the jelly was cooked too long.

Gummy: the jelly was overcooked or cooked too slowly.

Cloudy: the juice was not properly strained, or the jelly wasn't skimmed sufficiently.

Sugary: too much sugar was added, or the juice was overcooked before the sugar was added.

Jelly "weeps": either there was too much acid in the fruit or too little sugar was added. Too heavy a layer of paraffin or temperature extremes in storage will also cause "weeping."

If you are a novice, follow the recipes exactly. When you are familiar enough with the techniques of jelly-making to avoid the common pitfalls, it will be easy to create your own variations.

A NOTE ABOUT YIELDS

Because fruits vary so widely in juiciness, it is difficult to predict an accurate yield. As a general rule, 2 cups of prepared juicy fruit will yield 1 cup of juice. This, plus ¾ cup of sugar, will produce 1 eight-ounce glass of jelly. It is a good idea to have one extra container handy in case the yield is larger than anticipated.

Apple Jelly

Some favorite apples for jelly are Cortland, McIntosh, and Delicious.

4 or 5 medium-size ripe tart apples
1½ cups water (approximately)
2 cups sugar (approximately)

Remove stems, blossom ends, and cores of unpared apples. Cut into small pieces (4 or 5 apples make about 6 cups). Place in a kettle and barely cover with water. Cook 15 to 20 minutes over medium heat, stirring and mashing occasionally, until the fruit is soft. Strain through a dampened jelly bag or wet doubled cheesecloth; let drip a few hours or overnight. Measure the juice; there should be about 2 cups. Add 1 cup of sugar for each cup of juice. Boil rapidly, stirring occasionally, until a good jelly test results (page 14). Skim the froth. Pour the syrup into clean, dry jelly glasses. Seal (page 8). *Yield: 2 to 3 eight-ounce glasses.*

Mint Jelly

Prepare strained apple juice for Apple Jelly (above). Add 4 sprigs of fresh spearmint and/or other mints (do not use dried mints) to the juice. Boil 5 minutes. Remove the mint sprigs; proceed with the recipe for Apple Jelly.

The jelly may be tinted green, if desired, using about ½ teaspoon food color (add color a drop or two at a time to the syrup after the jelly stage is reached).

Rose Geranium Jelly

Prepare Apple Jelly (above). Place a rose geranium leaf in the bottom of each jelly glass before pouring the syrup into the glasses.

Spiced Apple Jelly

This is a spicy variation of plain Apple Jelly. It's wonderful on buttered toast and great with pancakes and waffles.

4 or 5 medium-size ripe tart apples
1½ cups water (approximately)
2 cups sugar (approximately)
1 cinnamon stick, broken in half, and ½ teaspoon whole cloves, tied in a cloth or cheesecloth bag
½ teaspoon ground nutmeg
½ teaspoon ground allspice

Remove stems, blossom ends, and cores of unpared apples and cut into small pieces (there should be about 6 cups). Put in a medium kettle and barely cover with water. Boil slowly over medium heat 15 to 20 minutes, stirring and mashing occasionally, until the fruit is soft. Strain through a dampened jelly bag or wet doubled cheesecloth and allow to drain for a few hours or overnight.

The following day, measure the juice; there should be about 2 cups. Combine juice in a small kettle with 1 cup of sugar for each cup of juice. Add the spices. Boil rapidly until a good jelly test results (page 14). Skim the froth. Remove the spice bag. Pour the syrup into clean, dry jelly glasses. Seal (page 8). *Yield: 2 to 3 eight-ounce glasses.*

Herb Jelly

This jelly is an accompaniment to meats. For the fresh herbs, use basil, marjoram, lemon thyme, mint, or peppermint; a combination of mint, marjoram, and burnet; or rose geranium and bay leaves, mixed with chopped lemon peel, sage, tarragon, or thyme.

2 pounds tart apples or crab apples
1½ cups water (approximately)
1 tablespoon white vinegar
4 sprigs fresh herbs (approximately)
3 cups sugar (approximately)

Remove the stems, blossom ends, and cores of the unpared apples. Cut into quarters, place in a kettle, and barely cover with water. Boil until soft, stirring and mashing occasionally. Strain through a dampened jelly bag or wet doubled cheesecloth; let drip a few hours or overnight.

Measure the juice; add the vinegar and 1 herb sprig for each cup of juice. Boil about 10 minutes. Add ¾ cup of sugar for each cup of juice, stirring until sugar dissolves. Boil the syrup until a good jelly test results (page 14). Remove the herbs. Skim the froth. Pour the syrup into clean, dry jelly glasses. Seal (page 8). *Yield: 3 to 4 eight-ounce glasses.*

Crab Apple Jelly

2 pounds ripe crab apples
1½ cups water (approximately)
4 cups sugar (approximately)

Remove the stems and blossom ends of the crab apples and cut into halves. Place in a kettle, barely cover with water, and cook about 25 minutes, or until the apples are tender. Strain through a dampened jelly bag or wet doubled cheesecloth; let drip a few hours or overnight.

Measure the juice and boil 5 minutes. Add 1 cup of sugar for each cup of juice; stir until the sugar dissolves. Boil rapidly until a good jelly test results (page 14). Skim the froth. Pour the syrup into clean, dry jelly glasses. Seal (page 8). *Yield: 2 to 3 eight-ounce glasses.*

Apple-Cranberry Jelly

2 pounds tart apples (6 or 7 medium)
1 pound cranberries (approximately)
2 to 3 cups water (approximately)
3 cups sugar (approximately)

Remove stems, blossom ends, and cores of unpared apples. Cut into small pieces and measure. Place in a kettle and add an equal amount of picked-over cranberries. Barely cover with water. Boil, covered, until the fruits are soft, about 20 minutes. Strain through a dampened jelly bag or wet doubled cheesecloth; let drip a few hours or overnight.

Return the pulp to the kettle, add water just to cover, and boil 30 minutes. Strain through a jelly bag or cheesecloth. Combine the two extractions, measure, and boil 5 minutes. Add ¾ cup of sugar for each cup of juice and stir until sugar dissolves. Boil rapidly until a good jelly test results (page 14). Skim the froth. Pour the syrup into clean, dry jelly glasses. Seal (page 8). *Yield: 5 to 6 eight-ounce glasses.*

Beach Plum Jelly

Beach plums grow wild along northeastern seashores. They are a small, round, sour fruit, pinky-purple or blue in color when ripe. They are ready for use in jelly and jam in August, when they ripen. When picking the fruit, always include some that are underripe to insure jelling. Beach Plum Jelly is delicious served with meats.

1 quart beach plums (include at least ½ cup underripe fruit)
1 cup water (approximately)
1½ cups sugar (approximately)

Place unpitted fruit in a kettle, barely cover with water, and boil, mashing occasionally, until the plums are quite soft, about 15 to 20 minutes. Strain through a dampened jelly bag or wet doubled cheesecloth; let drip a few hours or overnight.

Measure the juice and add ¾ cup of sugar for each cup of juice. Boil rapidly until a good jelly test results (page 14). Skim the froth. Pour the syrup into clean, dry jelly glasses. Seal (page 8). *Yield: 2 to 3 eight-ounce glasses.*

Paradise Jelly

4 large quinces
3 large tart apples (McIntosh are good)
2 cups cranberries
4 cups water (approximately)
3 to 3½ cups sugar (approximately)

Remove the blossom ends and cores of the quinces. Remove the stems, blossom ends, and cores of the unpared apples, and cut into pieces. Pick over the cranberries. Place the fruits in a large kettle and barely cover with water. Boil, stirring occasionally, until the fruits are mushy. Strain through a dampened jelly bag or wet doubled cheesecloth; let drip a few hours or overnight.

For a larger yield, return the drained pulp to the kettle, add water just to cover, and boil 30 minutes. Strain through a jelly bag or cheesecloth for a few hours. Combine the two extractions and boil 20 minutes. Skim the froth. Measure the juice and add 1 cup of sugar for each cup of juice. Boil until a good jelly test results (page 14). Skim the froth. Pour the syrup into clean, dry jelly glasses. Seal (page 8). *Yield: 4 to 5 eight-ounce glasses.*

Grape Jelly

Concord or Niagara grapes are good for this. Note: Overripe grapes make a syrupy jelly; underripe grapes give an inferior flavor.

2 pounds firm ripe grapes
6 cups water
3 cups sugar

Discard the grape stems and all green or decayed fruit. Place grapes in a kettle. Add 2 cups of the water and, mashing the fruit occasionally, boil slowly 10 minutes, or until the fruit is soft. Strain through a dampened jelly bag or one layer of wet cheesecloth for a few hours or overnight. Return the pulp to the kettle, add the remaining 4 cups of water, and simmer slowly 30 minutes. Strain through a dampened jelly bag or wet doubled cheesecloth; let drip a few hours or overnight.

Combine the two extractions and boil until reduced to 4 cups of juice. Add the sugar and boil rapidly until a good jelly test results (page 14). Skim the froth. Pour into clean, dry jelly glasses. Seal (page 8). *Yield: 4 eight-ounce glasses.*

Sea Grape Jelly

The sea grape is a wild fruit borne by the tree *Coccoloba uvifera*, which gets to be about twenty feet tall and grows in southern Florida as well as on the beaches of many Caribbean islands. The purple fruits look like grapes and grow in long clusters. This recipe is from Lala Jannes of Clearwater, Florida.

2 quarts sea grapes
2 cups sugar
2 tablespoons strained lemon juice

Place the sea grapes in a large kettle and barely cover with water. Simmer the fruit until loosened from the seeds. Place the pulp in a dampened jelly bag or wet doubled cheesecloth and let drain overnight.

The following day, measure 2 cups of juice and combine in a medium kettle with the sugar and lemon juice. (If you have more than 2 cups of juice you will need 1 cup of sugar and 1 tablespoon of strained lemon juice for each additional cup of fruit juice.) Boil slowly over medium heat, stirring occasionally, until a good jelly test results (page 14). Remove from the heat and skim the foam. Pour into clean, dry jelly glasses. Seal (page 8). *Yield: 3 six-ounce glasses.*

Scuppernong Grape Jelly

Nancy Phero, who lives in northern Florida, uses the fruits native to her area to make jams, jellies, preserves, and pickles of all sorts. Scuppernongs, a silvery amber-green variety of muscadine grape, grow wild around her home, and she sends her children out to pick them when she's ready to make jelly. The skins are so tough that you must mash them hard, very hard indeed, to extract the almost colorless juice. Because scuppernongs vary a great deal in ripeness, Nancy uses commercial pectin in her jelly. You can use other types of muscadines for this recipe.

3½ to 4 pounds scuppernong grapes
1 cup water
1 package powdered pectin
7 cups sugar
Red and blue food colors

Pick over the grapes carefully, discarding spoiled fruit. Place in a large bowl and crush thoroughly. Transfer to a large kettle, add the water, and bring to a simmer, adjusting the heat to maintain a low boil. Cook the grapes, stirring occasionally, until they are soft, about 10 to 15 minutes. Strain through a dampened jelly bag or wet doubled cheesecloth. Let drain overnight if the juice flows easily, or press through the bag until it pours very slowly.

The following day, measure 5 cups of juice. Combine in a medium kettle with the pectin, mixing well. Stirring constantly, bring to a rolling boil over high heat. Add the sugar and boil one minute, stirring constantly. Remove from the heat and skim the foam. For a bright purple color—like grape jelly—add red and blue food colors, a few drops at a time. Pour the syrup into clean, dry jelly glasses. Seal (page 8). *Yield: 8 to 9 eight-ounce glasses.*

Fox Grape Jelly

Fox grapes grow wild in many northern and eastern states. One area they thrive in is northern Florida, where their favorite habitats are fences and the bases of young trees. The grapes are dark purple, and tart and sweet at the same time. Many of our cultivated hardy varieties of grapes have been developed from this species. Jelly made from fox grapes is wonderfully tart, and particularly good when served as an accompaniment to meat and poultry.

3½ to 4 pounds fox grapes
1 cup water
1 package powdered pectin
7 cups sugar

Carefully pick over the grapes, discarding spoiled or very small, green, undeveloped fruit. Place the grapes in a large bowl and crush thoroughly. Transfer to a large kettle, add the water, and bring to a simmer, adjusting the heat to maintain a slow boil. Cook the grapes until they are thoroughly soft, about 10 to 15 minutes. Strain through a dampened jelly bag or wet doubled cheesecloth.

Measure 5 cups of juice and combine in a medium kettle with the pectin, mixing well. Stirring constantly, bring to a rolling boil over high heat. Add the sugar and boil 1 minute, stirring constantly. Remove from the heat and skim the froth. Pour the syrup into clean, dry jelly glasses. Seal (page 8). *Yield: 11 to 12 six-ounce glasses.*

Wine Orange Jelly

Use a mildly flavored honey, such as clover honey, rather than one with a strongly accented flavor. The wine can range from any pleasant domestic brand to a good French Chablis, left over from a meal.

1½ cups dry white wine
½ cup strained orange juice
1 teaspoon grated orange peel
2 tablespoons strained lemon juice
½ package powdered pectin (about 3 tablespoons)
4 cups honey

In a large kettle, combine the wine, orange juice and peel, lemon juice, and pectin. Bring to a full rolling boil, then stir in the honey. Let the mixture return to a full rolling boil and, stirring constantly, boil exactly 3 minutes. Remove from the heat and skim the froth. Pour the syrup into clean, dry jelly glasses and seal (page 8). *Yield: 6 eight-ounce glasses.*

Currant Jelly

1 quart ripe currants
4 cups water
4 cups sugar (approximately)

Pick over the currants. Place in a kettle, add 2 cups of the water, and boil slowly 10 to 15 minutes, mashing the fruit as it cooks. Strain through a dampened jelly bag or one layer of wet cheesecloth for a few hours or overnight. Return the pulp to the kettle, add the remaining 2 cups of water, and boil slowly 5 to 10 minutes. Strain through a dampened jelly bag or wet doubled cheesecloth.

Combine the two extractions and measure; add 1 cup of sugar for each cup of juice. Boil rapidly until a good jelly test results (page 14). Skim the froth. Pour into clean, dry jelly glasses. Seal (page 8). *Yield: 4 to 4½ eight-ounce glasses.*

Guava Jelly

Calamondins, a tropical fruit similar to guavas, are often used in this recipe instead of guavas.

1 pint guavas or calamondins
2 cups water
2 cups sugar

Remove the blossom ends of the fruit and slice thinly. Place in a kettle, add the water, and boil gently about 30 minutes, or until the fruit is very soft. Strain through a dampened jelly bag or wet doubled cheesecloth; let drip a few hours or overnight.

Add the sugar. Boil rapidly until a good jelly test results (page 14). Skim the froth. Pour into clean, dry jelly glasses. Seal (page 8). *Yield: 2 to 2½ eight-ounce glasses.*

Hawaiian Hot Pepper Jelly

Helen White, who has lived in Hawaii a long time, learned this recipe there; she serves the jelly most often with pork. Use commercial pectin in this recipe because the peppers contain no pectin. If powdered pectin is used, carefully follow the directions on the package.

¾ cup ground green peppers with juice
2 teaspoons ground red chili pepper
6½ cups sugar
1½ cups white vinegar
One 6-ounce bottle liquid pectin

Grind the peppers in a blender or put through a grinder, retaining the juice. Combine with the sugar and vinegar in a kettle and bring to a rolling boil. Boil, stirring, about 10 minutes, or until the peppers are tender. Remove from the heat and let sit 20 minutes. Return to heat and boil 2 minutes. Remove from the heat, add pectin, and stir 5 minutes. Pour syrup into clean, dry jelly glasses. Seal (page 8). *Yield: 6 to 7 eight-ounce glasses.*

Jams

Jams

Jams and jellies are made by the same process and with the same equipment, except for the cheesecloth or jelly bag (page 6). Among those fruits that make excellent jams are strawberries, raspberries, blackberries, loganberries, cherries, blueberries, currants, apricots, kumquats, rhubarb, plums, and peaches. Combinations of two or three fruits make superb, unusual jams. Not all jams, by the way, are sweet. Some jams, such as Red Pepper or Spiced Tomato, are accompaniments for meats.

Since jams are not turned out of their containers in perfectly molded shapes, as jelly can be, you may use all kinds of pretty containers. Look for interesting shapes. Save the small two- or three-ounce jars often used in packages of gift preserves: filled with your own homemade jams, these make very special gifts. Use leftover pickle and mayonnaise jars for preserves intended for family use. Make sure "found" jars have no cracks, or nicks on the rims. Ceramic and pottery jars may be used if they can be sealed easily with hot paraffin or plastic wrap. If you use the Boiling-Water Bath method of processing (page 9), use standard glass canning jars — "found" jars may not survive the processing.

MAKING JAM: GENERAL DIRECTIONS

1. Pick over the fruit and wash gently. Measure; for each cup of fruit add 2/3 cup of sugar. Combine in a kettle.

2. Stir the mixture over low heat until the sugar dissolves and the mixture comes to a boil. Boil rapidly, uncovered (to preserve the bright color and natural flavor of the fruit), until the jelly (or "sheeting") stage is reached (page 14). Stir often to prevent scorching.

3. Remove from heat and skim the froth. The brief cooling allows the fruit to distribute evenly throughout the syrup when the jam is poured into the glasses. Pour into clean, dry jelly glasses or canning jars. Seal with paraffin (page 8) or process jars 10 minutes in a Boiling-Water Bath (page 9).

4. If possible, store your jams in a cool, dark place, 30 to 50° F. If jams must be stored at warmer temperatures, try to use them up within six months. They won't spoil if kept longer, but they'll taste better if used within that period. This is one reason for making jellies and jams in small batches.

Strawberry Jam

6 cups firm ripe strawberries, hulled
5 cups sugar
1/3 cup strained lemon juice

Layer the berries and sugar in a large kettle. Let stand at room temperature 3 to 4 hours. Bring to a boil over medium-low heat, stirring carefully, until the sugar dissolves. Add the lemon juice and cook rapidly, uncovered, shaking the kettle occasionally, 10 to 12 minutes, or until the berries are plump and the syrup is thick. Pour into a shallow pan and skim the foam. Let stand, shaking the pan occasionally to allow berries to absorb the syrup (this should take from 20 to 40 minutes). When almost cool, pour into clean, dry jelly glasses or canning jars. Seal (page 8), and process 10 minutes in a Boiling-Water Bath (page 9). *Yield: 4 eight-ounce glasses.*

Raspberry Jam

1 quart raspberries
1¼ cups sugar (approximately)

Pick over the raspberries. Partially crush them in a large kettle. Heat slowly until the juice flows freely. Boil rapidly until the juice is reduced by about half. Measure the fruit; add 2/3 cup of sugar for each cup of fruit. Stir until the sugar dissolves. Boil rapidly until a good jelly test results (page 14). Remove from heat, skim the froth, and pour into clean, dry jelly glasses or canning jars. Seal (page 8), and process 10 minutes in a Boiling-Water Bath (page 9). *Yield: 2 to 3 eight-ounce glasses.*

Blueberry Jam

1 quart blueberries
1¼ cups sugar (approximately)

Pick over the blueberries. Partially crush them in a kettle. Heat slowly until the juice flows freely. Boil rapidly, stirring, until the juice is reduced by about half. Measure the fruit; add 2/3 cup of sugar for each cup of fruit. Stir until the sugar dissolves. Boil rapidly, stirring occasionally, until a good jelly test results (page 14). Remove from heat, skim the foam, and pour into clean, dry jelly glasses or canning jars. Seal (page 8), and process 10 minutes in a Boiling-Water Bath (page 9). *Yield: 2 to 3 eight-ounce glasses.*

Blueberry-Apple Jam

If you can get them, use wild blueberries and those crisp summer apples (often called Snow Apples) for this superb jam.

2 cups blueberries
2 medium-size tart apples
3 cups sugar
¼ cup water
1 teaspoon lemon juice

Pick over the blueberries. Remove stems, blossom ends, and cores of pared apples; coarsely chop, then measure 2 cupfuls. Combine sugar, water, and lemon juice in a kettle. Bring to a simmer over low heat, and stir in the blueberries and apples. Bring to a boil and cook about 20 minutes, stirring occasionally, until jam is thick and syrupy. Remove from heat, skim the foam, and pour into clean, dry jelly glasses or canning jars. Seal (page 8), and process 10 minutes in a Boiling-Water Bath (page 9). *Yield: 2 to 3 eight-ounce glasses.*

Wild Blackberry Jam

You can buy cultivated blackberries for preserving, but what is more pleasant than walking on country roads to pick juicy wild blackberries?

2 quarts wild blackberries
4 cups sugar (approximately)

Pick over the blackberries. Partially crush in a large kettle and bring to a boil. Simmer, covered, 10 minutes. Force through a sieve (or put through a food mill) to remove the seeds; discard the seeds. Measure the juice; add 1 cup of sugar for each cup of juice. Stir over medium-low heat until the sugar dissolves. Bring to a boil and boil rapidly, stirring occasionally, until a good jelly test results (page 14). Remove from heat, skim the foam, and pour into clean, dry jelly glasses or canning jars. Seal (page 8), and process 10 minutes in a Boiling-Water Bath (page 9). *Yield: 4 to 4½ eight-ounce glasses.*

Italian Prune Plum Jam

These dark, firm plums should be picked or used when the fruits are dead-ripe and their bloom is dusky. Bloom is the white cast on plum and grape skins, and looks rather like a fine powder.

1 quart Italian prune plums, pitted
1 cup water
2½ cups sugar (approximately)

Put the unpeeled plums in a kettle, add the water, and simmer until soft, mashing occasionally. Measure the fruit; add 2/3 cup of sugar for each cup of fruit. Stir until the sugar dissolves. Boil rapidly until a good jelly test results (page 14). Remove from heat, skim the foam, and pour into clean, dry jelly glasses or canning jars. Seal (page 8), and process 10 minutes in a Boiling-Water Bath (page 9). *Yield: 2 to 3 eight-ounce glasses.*

Bar-le-Duc

Bar-le-Duc is probably the most elegant of all jams. It is said that the food-conscious French once raised an obelisk to honor the creator of Bar-le-Duc. Originally, the jam was made with white currants, from which the seeds had been removed. The method was painstaking—a needle was inserted into each currant, and then the seed was pressed out. Today's versions are far less trouble, and use red currant juice, or a mixture of red and white currant juice, with raspberries. This is such a special treat that you might try to find small, two- or three-ounce jars for the jam and give it away only in tiny lots.

1 pint red currants (or a mixture of red and white)
1 quart raspberries
4½ cups sugar

Pick over the currants but do not remove the stems. Mash a few at a time in a kettle until all are pulpy. Simmer slowly, covered, until the currants look white, about 15 minutes. Strain through a coarse strainer, then let drip through a dampened jelly bag or wet doubled cheesecloth for a few hours or overnight.

Combine the raspberries and the currant juice and slowly heat to the boiling point. Add the sugar and boil rapidly until a good jelly test results (page 14). Let stand until almost cool. Skim off any foam and pour into clean, dry jelly glasses or canning jars. Seal (page 8). Do not process in a Boiling-Water Bath unless you feel you must. *Yield: 3 to 4 eight-ounce glasses.*

Old-Fashioned Fig Jam

Nobody makes fig jam anymore, but you should if figs are available to you at reasonable prices. Fig jam is especially fine with cream cheese on nut bread, or on ice cream.

1 quart dark ripe figs
2 cups sugar

Clip off the tough ends of the fig stems and place the fruit in a large bowl. Add the sugar, then mash firmly with a potato masher. Transfer the mixture to a large kettle and simmer very slowly over low heat about 20 to 30 minutes, stirring constantly, until the jam thickens and a good jelly test results (page 14). Remove from heat, skim the foam, and pour into clean, dry jelly glasses or canning jars. Seal (page 8), and process 10 minutes in a Boiling-Water Bath (page 9). *Yield: 2 to 3 eight-ounce glasses.*

Apricot Jam

Marcie Singhaus of Menlo Park, California, has an apricot tree on her patio. She loves it in every season, but especially at the time the fruit ripens and she can make jam.

1 pound ripe apricots, pitted
1½ cups sugar
½ orange, peeled, thinly sliced, and seeded
½ cup thinly sliced fresh pineapple

Put unpeeled apricots through a food chopper, using the finest blade. Combine with the sugar in a kettle and boil over medium heat 15 minutes, stirring often to prevent scorching. Add the orange and pineapple. Simmer about 45 minutes or until thick, stirring often. Remove from heat and let stand until almost cool. Skim off any foam and pour into clean, dry jelly glasses or canning jars. Seal (page 8), and process 10 minutes in a Boiling-Water Bath (page 9). *Yield: 3 to 4 eight-ounce glasses.*

Kumquat Jam

Really ripe kumquats have so much juice that the jam needs no water; thus their piquant flavor is preserved.

1½ pounds ripe kumquats, thinly sliced
3 cups sugar

Put the kumquats in a kettle, cover with the sugar, and simmer until thick, stirring occasionally, about 10 to 15 minutes. Remove from heat and let stand until almost cool. Pour into clean, dry jelly glasses or canning jars. Seal (page 8), and process 10 minutes in a Boiling-Water Bath (page 9). *Yield: 3 to 4 eight-ounce glasses.*

Deluxe Peach Jam

If you are fortunate enough to find Hale peaches, those white-fleshed triumphs of Connecticut growers, so much the better.

2½ cups peeled, quartered ripe peaches (reserve 1 peach stone)
1 cup cubed fresh pineapple (or drained canned pineapple)
3 cups sugar
¾ cup finely chopped pecans
Half of a 4-ounce bottle maraschino cherries, cut into halves
Syrup from one 4-ounce bottle maraschino cherries

In a kettle, mix the peaches and pineapple with the sugar; let stand 15 minutes. Crack a peach stone, remove the kernel, and add the kernel to the fruit mixture. Simmer over medium-low heat until the syrup is thick and clear. Add the nuts, cherries, and cherry syrup. Cook one minute longer. Remove from heat and let stand until almost cool. Skim off any foam and pour into clean, dry jelly glasses or canning jars. Seal (page 8), and process 10 minutes in a Boiling-Water Bath (page 9). *Yield: 3½ to 4 eight-ounce glasses.*

Gay's Strawberry-Rhubarb Jam

2 cups 1-inch pieces rhubarb
3 cups sugar
2 cups hulled strawberries
½ cup slivered blanched almonds

Cover the rhubarb with half the sugar; let stand 4 hours. Crush the strawberries in a deep kettle; add the remaining sugar and the sweetened rhubarb. Simmer over low heat, stirring, until the sugar dissolves.

Bring to a boil over medium heat and cook 15 minutes. Add the almonds. Continue cooking, stirring frequently, until a good jelly tests results (page 14). Remove from heat, skim the foam, and pour into clean, dry jelly glasses or canning jars. Seal (page 8), and process 10 minutes in a Boiling-Water Bath (page 9). *Yield: 3 to 4 eight-ounce glasses.*

Doris Smith's Rhubarb, Pineapple, and Strawberry Jam

This is the easiest to make of rhubarb jams. The flavors of these three fruits are not dissimilar and they blend beautifully in Doris's triple-treat recipe with its unusual ingredients.

5 cups 1-inch pieces rhubarb
One 8-ounce can crushed pineapple (undrained)
5 cups sugar
1 large or 2 small packages strawberry-flavored gelatin

Mix the rhubarb, pineapple, and sugar in a medium kettle. Stir often over low heat until the sugar dissolves, then simmer 20 minutes. Add the gelatin, stirring until completely dissolved. Without stirring, let the mixture return to a boil. Remove from heat, skim the foam, and pour at once into clean, dry jelly glasses or canning jars. Seal (page 8). *Yield: 4 to 5 eight-ounce glasses.*

Rhubarb and Ginger Jam

An old-fashioned and unusual combination, much beloved by our families.

2 pounds rhubarb, cut into 1-inch pieces
4 cups sugar
2 ounces crystallized ginger, cut into small pieces
Strained juice of 1 lemon

Put the rhubarb in a kettle and cover with the sugar. Add the ginger and lemon juice. Simmer one hour, stirring occasionally, until a good jelly test results (page 14). Pour into clean, dry jelly glasses or canning jars. Seal (page 8), and process 10 minutes in a Boiling-Water Bath (page 9). *Yield: 4 to 5 eight-ounce glasses.*

Frances Chrystie's Rose Hip Jam

On a warm, sunny, approaching-autumn day, just after the first frost, Frances goes down the path to her beach and gathers rose hips ripening on *Rosa rugosa* brambles that grow wild along reaches of Long Island, New York. Rose hips are round, satiny fruits filled with seeds. Frances picks the largest she can find.

4 cups rose hips
1 cup water
Sugar

Combine rose hips and water in a kettle. Cover and simmer over medium heat until the fruit is very tender, about 30 minutes. Force the pulp through a sieve and measure; for each cup of fruit, add 1 cup of sugar. Simmer the mixture until thick, about 10 to 15 minutes. Remove from heat, skim the foam, and pour into clean, dry jelly glasses or canning jars. Seal (page 8), and process 10 minutes in a Boiling-Water Bath (page 9). *Yield: 2 to 4 eight-ounce glasses.*

Pineapple Jam

This delicious sweet-sour jam also makes a great filling just as is for a baked pie shell. Top with ice cream and you have a luscious calorie-laden dessert. The flavor of ripe pineapple is better than that of a not-quite-ripe fruit, so choose your specimen carefully. A pineapple usually has developed its full flavor if the inner leaves of the rosette at the top of the fruit are loose and pull out easily. Test before you buy.

1 large ripe pineapple
2½ cups sugar
1 cup water
½ lemon, thinly sliced and seeded

Slice the top off the pineapple about 1 inch below the base of the leaves. Slice off about ¼ inch of the bottom. Peel the fruit, using a large, sharp knife. Use a potato peeler to remove the eyes that remain after the fruit is peeled. Slice the pineapple flesh away from the core (the hard, pale central section), then chop the flesh finely. Combine the chopped pineapple, sugar, water, and lemon in a medium kettle. Stir constantly over medium-low heat until the sugar dissolves. When the mixture begins to boil slowly, raise the heat to medium-high. Boil slowly until the jam thickens, about 30 minutes, stirring frequently to prevent scorching. Remove from heat, skim the foam, and pour into clean, dry jelly glasses or canning jars. Seal (page 8), and process 10 minutes in a Boiling-Water Bath (page 9). *Yield: about 3 eight-ounce glasses.*

Waste-Not Want-Not Jam

Here's a recipe to use up those odds and ends of fruit going to waste in your fruit bowl. It's also a good recipe to use when you find tempting but costly fruit at the market and can't afford to put up a whole batch: just combine a small amount of the expensive treat with your leftover fruits to make this mixed fruit jam. If the fruits you are using have a lot of large, heavy pits (peaches, for instance), allow 2½ to 3½ pounds of fruit instead of the 2 pounds the recipe calls for.

2 pounds mixed fruits (strawberries, plums, blackberries, peaches, nectarines, etc.)
3 cups sugar
1 tablespoon strained lemon juice

Peel the fruits and remove the stems, blossom ends, cores, and/or pits as necessary. Cut the fruits into medium cubes and crush together in a medium kettle, releasing the juices. Measure the pulp and juice; there should be about 4 cups. (Add proportionately less sugar if it falls short of 4 cups.) Add the sugar and lemon juice to the kettle and stir over low heat until the sugar dissolves. Raise the heat and boil slowly, stirring often, until the mixture just reaches the jelly stage (page 14). Remove from heat, skim the foam, and let stand about 5 minutes to distribute the fruit evenly. Pour into clean, dry jelly glasses or canning jars. Seal (page 8), and process 10 minutes in a Boiling-Water Bath (page 9). *Yield: 3 eight-ounce glasses.*

Carrot Jam

This unusual jam doesn't remind you at all of the carrots with which it is made. Late-season carrots — the dark-orange, dense, sweet carrots that come onto the market in fall — make the best jam.

2 cups grated carrots (3 or 4 medium-large)
1½ cups sugar
Strained juice and grated peel of 1 lemon
¼ teaspoon each ground cloves, allspice, and cinnamon

Combine all the ingredients in a medium kettle. Stir constantly over low heat until the sugar dissolves. Bring to a slow boil, reduce heat immediately, and simmer very slowly, stirring constantly, until the jam thickens, about 15 to 20 minutes. Remove from heat, skim the foam, and pour into clean, dry jelly glasses or canning jars. Seal (page 8), and process 10 minutes in a Boiling-Water Bath (page 9). *Yield: 3 to 4 eight-ounce glasses.*

Red Pepper Jam

6 large sweet red peppers, seeded
½ teaspoon salt
¾ cup cider vinegar
¼ cup water
½ lemon, cut into quarters
1½ cups sugar

Put peppers through a food chopper, using the finest blade. Sprinkle with salt; let stand 3 to 4 hours. Drain well and combine in a kettle with the vinegar, water, and lemon pieces. Simmer about 30 minutes. Remove the lemon and add the sugar. Simmer until quite thick, stirring often, 15 to 20 minutes. Remove from heat and let stand until almost cool. Skim the foam and pour into clean, dry jelly glasses or canning jars. Seal (page 8), and process 10 minutes in a Boiling-Water Bath (page 9). *Yield: 3 to 4 eight-ounce glasses.*

Green Tomato Jam

Green Tomato Jam is excellent served with meat or curry.

2 pounds green tomatoes
Grated peel and strained juice of 2 large lemons
1 teaspoon ground ginger
Water
4 cups sugar

Cut off and discard stem ends of tomatoes; chop finely. Combine in a kettle with the peel and juice of the lemons and the ginger. Add barely enough water to cover the bottom of the kettle. Simmer one hour, stirring occasionally. Add the sugar and cook until thick, stirring often. Remove from heat, skim the foam, and pour into clean, dry jelly glasses or canning jars. Seal (page 8), and process 10 minutes in a Boiling-Water Bath (page 9). *Yield: 4 to 5 eight-ounce glasses.*

Spiced Tomato Jam

2 pounds firm ripe tomatoes
1 large sour apple
1 cinnamon stick, broken in half, and ½ teaspoon whole allspice, tied in a cloth or cheesecloth bag
½ teaspoon salt
2 cups firmly packed brown sugar
3 tablespoons lemon juice

Peel and core the tomatoes; cut into quarters. Peel, core, and dice the apple. Combine all the ingredients in a kettle and stir over low heat until the sugar dissolves. Stirring often, simmer about one hour or until thick. Remove from heat and let stand until almost cool. Remove the spice bag. Skim the foam and pour into clean, dry jelly glasses or canning jars. Seal (page 8), and process 10 minutes in a Boiling-Water Bath (page 9). *Yield: 4 to 5 eight-ounce glasses.*

Marmalades, Conserves, Preserves, & Butters

Marmalades & Such

A tale brought to us from Scotland by young Kris Littledale concerns the way in which marmalade got its name. It seems that Mary, Queen of Scots, fell ill and nothing helped her. Finally, her nurse insisted that she try toast with a jelly made from bitter oranges, peel and all. The Queen liked it and recovered. The bitter orange jelly became known as "Mary-malade" (*malade* is French for "ill"), which was corrupted to "marmalade." We now use the name for all jellylike mixtures containing citrus fruits.

Recipes for conserves begin on page 33. Like jams, they are delicious on breakfast breads but many are also excellent accompaniments for meat and poultry dishes. Preserves, page 36, utilize a wide variety of fruits (and even tomatoes!); serve them as condiments or change-of-pace desserts. We also have included some old-fashioned tutti-frutti concoctions. Fruit butters, page 40, recall a breakfast-table favorite of many generations of Americans.

Orange Marmalade

In England and Scotland, orange marmalade is usually made with bitter Seville oranges from Spain, but great marmalades can be made with navel oranges, limes, lemons, or grapefruit, always available in this country.

6 navel oranges
1 lemon
4 cups water (approximately)
4 cups sugar (approximately)

Peel the rinds from the oranges and lemon. Remove and discard the white membrane and seeds. Cut the flesh into small pieces. Using scissors or a single-edge razor blade, cut the peel into slivers—the smaller, the better. Mix the flesh and the peel. Measure; add 1 cup of water for each cup of fruit. Let stand overnight.

The following day, place mixture in a shallow pan and boil rapidly 20 minutes. Measure; add 1 cup of sugar for each cup of fruit mixture. Boil 30 minutes, stirring constantly with a wooden spoon. Turn into clean, dry jelly glasses or canning jars. Seal (page 8), and process 10 minutes in a Boiling-Water Bath (page 9). *Yield: 5 to 6 eight-ounce glasses.*

Grapefruit Marmalade

Substitute 2 large grapefruit for 3 of the oranges in the Orange Marmalade recipe (above); proceed with the recipe.

Emily Gay's Amber Marmalade

1 orange
1 lemon
1 grapefruit
4 cups water (approximately)
4 cups sugar (approximately)

Shave unpeeled fruit very thinly, discarding cores and seeds. (Or as a time-saver, cut up the fruit, discarding seeds and cores, and put through a food chopper, using a coarse blade.) Measure the fruit; add 3 times as much water. Let stand overnight.

The following day, place in a kettle, bring to a simmer, and cook 10 minutes. Let stand another night. The second morning, measure; add 1 cup of sugar for each cup of fruit. Boil steadily, stirring once in a while, until a good jelly test results (page 14). This will take about 1½ to 2 hours. Remove from heat, skim the foam, and turn into clean, dry jelly glasses or canning jars. Seal (page 8), and process 10 minutes in a Boiling-Water Bath (page 9). *Yield: 5 eight-ounce glasses.*

Lime Marmalade

3 limes (Key limes are excellent)
1 lemon
2½ cups water (approximately)
3 cups sugar (approximately)

Slice unpeeled fruit very thinly, discarding cores and seeds. (Or as a time-saver, cut up the fruit, discarding seeds and cores, and put through a food chopper, using a coarse blade.) Measure the fruit; add twice as much water. Boil slowly, covered, about 15 minutes. Measure; add 1 cup of sugar for each cup of fruit. Boil until a good jelly test results (page 14). Remove from heat, skim the foam, and turn into clean, dry jelly glasses or canning jars. Seal (page 8), and process 10 minutes in a Boiling-Water Bath (page 9). *Yield: 3 six-ounce glasses.*

Cherry-Pineapple Marmalade

1½ pounds sour cherries
1 medium pineapple
1 large orange
3 cups sugar

Remove the stems from the cherries and pit them. Chop the cherries, then measure; you will need 3 cups. Peel and core the pineapple. Chop finely and measure 3 cups. Cut the orange in half and remove the seeds. Cut into very fine slivers (include the peel).

Combine all the ingredients in a medium kettle and cook, stirring, over medium-low heat, until the sugar dissolves. Raise the heat and boil rapidly, stirring occasionally, until thick or until a good jelly test results (page 14), about 12 minutes. Remove from heat, skim the foam, and turn into clean, dry jelly glasses or canning jars. Seal (page 8), and process 15 minutes in a Boiling-Water Bath (page 9). *Yield: 4 to 5 eight-ounce glasses.*

Cantaloupe-Peach Marmalade

3 oranges, halved and seeded
2 lemons, halved and seeded
4 cups finely diced ripe cantaloupe
4 cups diced peeled peaches
6 cups sugar
3 or 4 maraschino cherries, cut into halves

Put the unpeeled oranges and lemons through a food chopper. Combine the cantaloupe and peaches in a kettle and simmer 2 minutes. Add the oranges and lemons and stir in the sugar. Stirring frequently, simmer over medium heat until the mixture thickens and a good jelly test results (page 14). Pour into clean, dry jelly glasses or canning jars. Drop half a cherry into each. Seal (page 8), and process 10 minutes in a Boiling-Water Bath (page 9). *Yield: 6 to 8 eight-ounce glasses.*

Guava Marmalade

Lala Jannes, who lives in Clearwater, Florida, finds that the small red-fleshed guavas available there are ideal for this marmalade. You may need as much as 4 cups of fresh guavas to make the 2 cups of guava pulp called for in the recipe. Select only very ripe guavas. Try this marmalade on French toast, and garnish with sour cream.

1 quart guavas (approximately)
¼ cup water
1½ cups sugar
¼ cup strained lemon juice

Remove the seeds from the guavas and slice the fruit very thinly. Place in a small kettle, add the water, and boil slowly over medium heat until the fruit is soft, about 20 to 30 minutes. Stir the pulp well and measure 2 cups. (If you have more than 2 cups of pulp you will need 3/4 cups of sugar and 2 tablespoons of strained lemon juice for each additional cup of pulp.) Combine the pulp, sugar, and lemon juice in the kettle. Boil slowly over medium heat, stirring often, until thickened, about 30 to 40 minutes. Pour into clean, dry jelly glasses or canning jars. Seal (page 8), and process 10 minutes in a Boiling-Water Bath (page 9). *Yield: about 2 eight-ounce glasses.*

Barbara's Carrot Marmalade

Try this, using fairly large carrots—it's terrific!

1 cup shredded or ground carrots
1 cup very thin unpeeled lemon slices
Peel of ½ medium orange
2 cups water
2 cups sugar
¼ cup maraschino cherries, cut into halves

Combine carrots, lemon slices, orange peel, and water. Let stand overnight. The following day, bring the mixture to a simmer and cook, covered, 20 minutes. Add the sugar, stirring until it dissolves. Simmer, stirring constantly, until a good jelly test results (page 14). Remove from heat and stir in the cherries. Pour into clean, dry jelly glasses or canning jars. Seal (page 8), and process 10 minutes in a Boiling-Water Bath (page 9). *Yield: 2 to 3 eight-ounce glasses.*

Tomato Marmalade

Use as a delicious spread for toast, or as a relish for meats.

2½ pounds ripe tomatoes (about 7 or 8 medium)
1 lemon, thinly sliced and seeded
½ teaspoon ground ginger
4 cups sugar

Peel the tomatoes and chop coarsely. Combine with the lemon and ginger in a kettle and bring to a boil. Reduce heat and simmer, uncovered, one hour. Stir in the sugar. Stirring frequently, simmer until thick about 25 to 30 minutes, or until a good jelly test results (page 14). Turn into clean, dry jelly glasses or canning jars. Seal (page 8), and process 10 minutes in a Boiling-Water Bath (page 9). *Yield: 3½ eight-ounce glasses.*

Pink Rhubarb Conserve

You must use red-skinned rhubarb to have the right color for this conserve. Save your green rhubarb for other concoctions.

1 lemon
2 cups 1-inch pieces red ripe rhubarb
2 cups sugar
¼ cup coarsely chopped walnuts or almonds
¼ cup seedless white raisins

Squeeze the lemon; strain and reserve the juice. Simmer the peel in water to cover until soft. Scoop out and discard the white pulp. Using scissors or a razor blade, cut the peel into fine slivers. In a bowl, pour the lemon juice over the rhubarb; add lemon peel and sugar. Let stand overnight.

The following day, transfer to a deep kettle and boil about 20 to 30 minutes, stirring occasionally, until the mixture is thick. Add the nuts and raisins and boil 5 minutes longer. Pour into clean, dry jelly glasses or canning jars. Seal (page 8), and process 10 minutes in a Boiling-Water Bath (page 9). *Yield: 2 to 2½ eight-ounce glasses.*

Spring Fruit Conserve

1 cup shredded fresh pineapple and juice
1 cup diced rhubarb
Few grains salt
2½ cups sugar
2 cups hulled strawberries

In a kettle, simmer pineapple in its own juice 10 minutes. Add the rhubarb, salt, and ½ cup of the sugar; simmer 5 minutes. Add remaining sugar and bring to a boil. Add the strawberries and boil, stirring frequently, about 30 minutes, until thick and translucent. Turn into clean, dry jelly glasses or canning jars. Seal (page 8), and process 10 minutes in a Boiling-Water Bath (page 9). *Yield: 2 to 3 eight-ounce glasses.*

Strawberry-Rhubarb Conserve

This is the classic recipe for Strawberry-Rhubarb Conserve. Red rhubarb makes the prettiest preserves, and the best. (Green rhubarb is usually used for making pies.)

1 pound rhubarb
1 pint hulled strawberries
4 cups sugar

Remove the leaves from the rhubarb and the coarse tips of the stalks and cut into 2-inch lengths. Measure 3 cups. Slice the strawberries and measure 2 cups. Combine with the rhubarb and sugar in a medium kettle. Stir gently over low heat until the sugar dissolves. Raise the heat to medium-high and cook rapidly, stirring often, until the conserve thickens, about 1½ to 2 hours. Remove from heat, skim the foam, and turn into clean, dry half-pint canning jars. Seal (page 8), and process 10 minutes in a Boiling-Water Bath (page 9). *Yield: 2 pints.*

Baked Rhubarb and Strawberry Conserve

The prebaking of these fruits blends the flavors into a piquant medley like no other.

12 cups finely cut rhubarb
12 cups hulled small strawberries
One 10-ounce can sliced pineapple, drained
½ cup red currants (if available)
Thin yellow peel of 1 lemon
Strained juice of ½ lemon
8 cups sugar

Heat oven to 375° F. Combine all the ingredients in a large oblong glass baking dish and bake one hour. Turn mixture into a large kettle and boil 20 to 30 minutes, or until a good jelly test results (page 14). Turn into clean, dry jelly glasses or canning jars. Seal (page 8), and process 10 minutes in a Boiling-Water Bath (page 9). *Yield: 6 eight-ounce glasses.*

Blueberry Conserve

1 quart blueberries (wild, if possible)
4 cups sugar
2 cups water
½ lemon, thinly sliced and seeded
½ medium orange, thinly sliced and
   seeded
½ cup seedless golden raisins

Remove the blueberry stems and set the berries aside. Combine the sugar and water in a medium kettle over medium heat, stirring occasionally to prevent the sugar from scorching on the sides of the kettle. When the syrup reaches a boil, add the lemon and orange slices and the raisins to the kettle; reduce heat and simmer 5 minutes. Add the blueberries and boil slowly over medium-high heat, stirring often to prevent scorching, until the mixture thickens, about 30 minutes. Pour into clean, dry, hot half-pint canning jars. Seal (page 8), and process 10 minutes in a Boiling-Water Bath (page 9). *Yield: about 2 pints.*

Cherry-Raspberry Conserve

1 quart fully ripe raspberries
1 to 1½ pounds sweet black cherries
4 cups sugar

Force the raspberries through a sieve or put through a food mill to remove seeds. Measure out 3 cups and set aside.

Remove the stems and pits from the cherries and measure 3 heaping cups. Put the cherries in a medium kettle and simmer over low heat, stirring occasionally, until tender, about 5 to 10 minutes. Add the raspberry pulp and the sugar, and stir over low heat until the sugar dissolves. Stirring often to prevent scorching, boil slowly until thickened, about 30 minutes. Turn into clean, dry, hot half-pint canning jars. Seal (page 8), and process 10 minutes in a Boiling-Water Bath (page 9). *Yield: 2 pints.*

Black Cherry Conserve

2 medium oranges
¼ cup water (approximately)
1 quart large, ripe, sweet black cherries
3½ cups sugar
6 tablespoons strained lemon juice
6 whole cloves and 1 half-inch piece stick
   cinnamon, tied in a cheesecloth bag

Cut the unpeeled oranges into very thin slices. Remove the seeds. Place the orange slices in a medium kettle over low heat, and add just enough water to prevent the fruit from scorching until it renders its own juices. Raise the heat to medium-low and cook, stirring occasionally, until the fruit is barely tender, about 10 minutes. Remove from the heat.

Remove the stems and pits from the cherries and add to the kettle along with the sugar, lemon juice, and spice bag. Boil slowly over medium heat, stirring often, until the juices are thick and clear, about 20 to 30 minutes. Remove the spice bag. Turn into clean, dry half-pint canning jars. Seal (page 8), and process 10 minutes in a Boiling-Water Bath (page 9). *Yield: 1 pint.*

Gooseberry Conserve

1½ quarts gooseberries
1 cup seedless golden raisins
1 medium orange, seeded and chopped
4 cups sugar
¼ cup water

Remove the gooseberry stems (tedious, but worthwhile) and the blossom ends. Combine all the ingredients in a medium kettle and stir over medium-low heat until the sugar dissolves. Raise the heat to medium and boil slowly, stirring frequently, until the mixture almost reaches the jelly stage (page 14). Pour into clean, dry half-pint canning jars. Seal (page 8), and process 10 minutes in a Boiling-Water Bath (page 9). *Yield: about 3 pints.*

Cranberry Conserve

This is a variation of that delicious orange-cranberry relish recipe printed on cranberry boxes. Process in a Boiling-Water Bath and store on a handy shelf, ready to use at the first hint of a turkey cooking.

1 medium orange
2 cups water
4 cups fresh cranberries
3 cups sugar
½ cup seedless raisins
½ cup walnuts or pecans, coarsely
   chopped

Chop the unpeeled orange very finely, discarding the seeds. Combine with the water in a medium kettle and boil rapidly over medium-high heat until the peel is tender, about 20 minutes. Meanwhile, remove the stems from the cranberries. Add the cranberries to the kettle, along with the sugar and the raisins. Lower the heat, and bring the mixture slowly to a boil, stirring often until the sugar dissolves. Raise the heat to medium-high and boil rapidly, stirring often, to about 215° F. on a jelly thermometer or until a sheeting test shows almost done (page 14). This should take about 8 minutes. Add the nuts during the last 5 minutes of cooking time. Turn into clean, dry half-pint canning jars. Seal (page 8), and process 10 minutes in a Boiling-Water Bath (page 9). *Yield: 2 pints.*

Apricot-Orange Conserve

4 pounds ripe apricots
6 medium oranges
6 cups sugar
1 tablespoon strained lemon juice
1 cup walnuts, quartered (optional)

Cut the apricots from the pits in quarter segments. Grate the peel (include the white part) from one orange; there should be 4 level tablespoonfuls. Peel 2 more oranges;

discard the peel. Slice those 3 oranges very thinly and discard the seeds. Cut and juice the remaining 3 oranges; strain the juice.

In a medium kettle, combine the apricot quarters; orange juice, peel, and slices; sugar; and lemon juice. Stir over low heat until the sugar dissolves. Raise heat and boil rapidly, stirring occasionally, until thick. When the mixture is almost thick enough to mound on a spoon, add the nuts and cook 5 minutes longer. Turn into clean, dry jelly glasses or half-pint canning jars. Seal (page 8), and process 10 minutes in a Boiling-Water Bath (page 9). *Yield: 5 pints.*

Peach Conserve

1 medium orange
½ lemon
½ pound seedless golden raisins
2½ pounds ripe peaches
4½ cups sugar
1 cup whole walnuts

Grate the peel of the orange and the lemon, using the coarse side of a grater. Do this carefully to avoid breaking the inner white skin of the fruits. Cut the orange in half. Juice the orange and lemon halves thoroughly on a reamer, retaining all the juice and whatever pulp falls into the juice. Discard the seeds. Put the juice, grated peel, and pulp in a medium kettle.

Grind the raisins to small pieces in a food mill. Peel, halve, and pit the peaches, and cut the flesh into medium cubes. Add the ground raisins and peach cubes to the kettle, along with the sugar. Stir the mixture over low heat until the sugar dissolves. Continue to simmer over low heat, stirring often, until the mixture thickens. Add the walnuts and simmer 10 minutes longer. Pour into clean, dry half-pint canning jars. Seal (page 8), and process 10 minutes in a Boiling-Water Bath (page 9). *Yield: about 2 to 2½ pints.*

Grace Pratt's Plum Gumbo

Grace uses this gumbo to glaze ham before baking; it is good to serve with other meats as well.

1 pound seedless raisins
2 medium oranges, cut up and seeded
2 pounds ripe plums, pitted and thinly
　sliced
3 cups sugar

Put the raisins and unpeeled oranges through a coarse blade of a food chopper. Combine with remaining ingredients in a kettle. Stirring occasionally, cook until thick, about one hour. Pour into clean, dry jelly glasses or canning jars. Seal (page 8), and process 10 minutes in a Boiling-Water Bath (page 9). *Yield: 4 to 5 eight-ounce glasses.*

Brandied Peaches

5 pounds small peaches
5 cups sugar
5 cups water
12 tablespoons (¾ cup) brandy

Remove the stems from the peaches and drop them into a lot of boiling water for one minute. Transfer to cold water and quickly peel off the skins. Combine the sugar and 5 cups water in a medium kettle and bring to a boil. Add the peaches and simmer 5 minutes, turning the fruit often so that all sides are in the syrup.

Remove the peaches with a slotted spoon and pack in clean, dry pint canning jars, filling them to within ½ inch of the rims. Add 2 tablespoons brandy to each jar, then fill with boiling syrup to within ¼ inch of the rims. Seal (page 8), and process 15 minutes in a Boiling-Water Bath (page 9). *Yield: 6 pints.*

Ann Le Moine's Jubilee Brandied Cherries

This is impressive served either hot as a gala winter dessert or ice-cold as a summer treat. It can be offered in punch cups, plain or with whipped cream, or poured over vanilla ice cream, a slice of pound cake, or a dish of rice pudding. The preserves are also delicious served with meat. Canned stewed sour cherries are sold in most supermarkets. They should be of the deep red variety; if not, add food color.

2 cups drained stewed sour cherries
1 or 2 cups sugar*
⅛ teaspoon salt
2 cups brandy
2 cinnamon sticks (optional)
Cornstarch (optional)

In a small kettle, mix the cherries, sugar, and salt. Stir over medium heat until the sugar dissolves. Remove from heat and let cool. Add the brandy. Pour into half-pint or pint-size glass containers and, if desired, insert 1 cinnamon stick in each jar. Cover with lids. Serve after 2 weeks. The cherries will keep indefinitely in the refrigerator. *Yield: 1 to 1½ pints.*

If you wish to serve as an accompaniment to meat, thicken the syrup with a little cornstarch, since the syrup is rather thin. Add 1 tablespoon of cornstarch for each ¼ cup of syrup. Place in a saucepan over medium-low heat with the cherries and heat, stirring, until the mixture thickens.

*When Ann makes these preserves to serve with meat, she uses 1 cup of sugar; when she intends to use them primarily for desserts, she uses 2 cups of sugar.

Francesca Morris's Brandied Fruit

The origins of tutti-frutti, or brandied fruit, are so ancient that we don't know where this gloriously flavorful concoction was first made. There are several recipes current, and none of them is like another. All the recipes agree, however, that the brandy should be good brandy. The action of sugar and brandy in tutti-frutti makes processing unnecessary. Fran makes her recipe in a two-quart apothecary jar over a period of six weeks.

1 pint good brandy
1 cup cut-up pineapple
1 cup cut-up peeled peaches
1 cup maraschino cherries
3 cups sugar

Pour the brandy into a 2-quart apothecary jar or other glass or porcelain container. Add 1 cup of the fruits — any one of the three kinds of fruit can be used first. Add 1 cup of the sugar and stir well. Cover the jar and allow to rest at room temperature for 2 weeks. You must not add the ingredients before 2 weeks are up, but you also must not wait longer than a total of 17 days before adding the second cup of fruit.

On the fourteenth to seventeenth day, no earlier or later, add 1 cup of another of the listed fruits, along with 1 cup of the sugar. Mix well, cover the container, and allow to rest 2 weeks, as before.

On the fourteenth to seventeenth day, no earlier or later, add the third, and last, cup of fruit, along with the last cup of sugar. Mix well and cover again. Allow to rest 2 weeks. The tutti-frutti is then ready to eat. *Yield: about 1 quart.*

Thalia's Tutti-Frutti

Thalia's recipe is intended to be made over the several weeks of the fruit season and can be processed in a Boiling-Water Bath when it is finished. Her tutti-frutti is mixed in a stone jar, six quarts or more in size.

1 quart good brandy
1 quart strawberries
1 quart cherries
1 quart raspberries
1 quart cut-up peeled apricots or peaches
1 quart cut-up pineapple
20 cups sugar

Pour the brandy into a 6-quart stone or glass jar, cover it tightly, and set in a cool place. As the fruits come into season, peel and pit or hull the fruits. Measure 4 cups of fruit and add to the brandy along with 4 cups of sugar. Store the jar in a very cool place, preferably not above 45° F. Stir the contents daily until all the fruits and sugar have been added.

When all the fruits have been added, you may, if you wish, pack the tutti-frutti into clean, dry half-pint or pint canning jars, filling to within ½ inch of the rims, then pour in the liquid to within ¼ inch of the rims. Seal (page 8), and process 10 minutes in a Boiling-Water Bath (page 9). *Yield: about 12 pints.*

Golden Gate Spiced Loquats

You'll find loquats at specialty markets on and off during the year. Choose fruit that is freshly picked and not overripe.

1 quart loquats
1½ cups sugar
2 lemons, thinly sliced and seeded
2 cups cider vinegar
1½ tablespoons ground cinnamon
1½ teaspoons ground cloves

Remove stems and blossom ends from the unpeeled loquats. Combine with remaining ingredients in a kettle and boil slowly, stirring frequently, until fruit is tender. Pack into clean, dry jelly glasses or canning jars, filling them to within ½ inch of the rims. Fill with cooking liquid to within ¼ inch of rims. Seal (page 8), and process 10 minutes in a Boiling-Water Bath (page 9). *Yield: 3 to 4 eight-ounce glasses.*

Florence Eldredge's Spiced Crab Apples

These rosy fruits enhance any meat platter.

2 pounds crab apples
4 cups sugar
2 cups vinegar
1 cup water
4 cinnamon sticks
8 whole cloves

Leave the stems on, but remove the blossom ends of the crab apples. Prick the skins with a fork to prevent bursting. Combine the remaining ingredients in a kettle and heat over low heat until the sugar dissolves, about 5 minutes. Add the crab apples and simmer 10 minutes. Pack the crab apples into 4 clean, dry pint canning jars, filling them to within ½ inch of the rims. Fill the jars with hot syrup to within ¼ inch of the rims. Seal (page 8), and process 10 minutes in a Boiling-Water Bath (page 9). *Yield: 4 pints.*

Apple-Ginger Preserve

This is an old-fashioned recipe for apple preserves.

5 cups tart apples (4 to 6 medium)
5 cups sugar
Peel of 1 lemon
One 2-inch piece fresh gingerroot

Peel, core, and chop the apples. Measure 5 cups and put in a medium kettle. Add the sugar. Cut the lemon peel into the thinnest possible strips and add to the kettle along with the gingerroot. Place the kettle over low heat. As the sugar dissolves, stir very gently to avoid mashing the apples. Stirring gently but often, simmer 2 hours or until the apples are translucent. Keep the simmer very low (the surface should barely bubble) or the apples will break. Remove gingerroot and pour into clean, dry, hot half-pint canning jars. Seal (page 8), and process 10 minutes in a Boiling-Water Bath (page 9). *Yield: about 1½ pints.*

Barbara Pond's Citron Melon Preserve

This white-fleshed preserving melon is sometimes called White Gourd of India.

2 pounds citron melon
4 cups sugar
2 cups water
1 large or 2 small lemons, thinly sliced
¼ teaspoon ground ginger or 2 tablespoons finely chopped crystallized ginger

Peel the melon and remove seeds. Cut into 1-inch cubes. Combine the sugar and water in a kettle and boil until reduced to a thick syrup. Add the melon, lemon, and ginger. Simmer over low heat, stirring often, until the melon is tender, about 20 to 30 minutes. Turn into clean, dry jelly glasses or half-pint canning jars. Seal (page 8), and process 10 minutes in a Boiling-Water Bath (page 9). *Yield: 4 to 6 eight-ounce glasses.*

Fig Preserves

This is less sweet than Old-Fashioned Fig Jam (page 25). Use ripe red or white figs.

1 quart ripe figs (about 2 pounds)
3½ cups sugar
2 tablespoons strained lemon juice
1½ quarts hot water
1 lemon, very thinly sliced and seeded

Peel the figs and clip off the tough ends of the stems. Set aside. In a medium kettle, combine the sugar, lemon juice, and hot water. Place over low heat and stir often until the sugar dissolves. Add the whole figs and raise the heat to medium-high. Boil rapidly 10 minutes, stirring often. Add the unpeeled lemon slices to the cooking figs and continue to boil rapidly 10 to 15 minutes longer, or until the figs begin to look translucent. Remove from heat, cover the kettle, and let the figs stand 12 to 24 hours at room temperature. Pack into clean, dry, hot half-pint canning jars, filling them to within ½ inch of the rims. Fill with liquid to within ¼ inch of the rims. Seal (page 8), and process 30 minutes in a Boiling-Water Bath (page 9). *Yield: about 2½ pints.*

Whole Strawberry Preserves

1 quart firm ripe strawberries, hulled
3 cups sugar

Put the strawberries in a kettle with 1 cup of the sugar and boil 5 minutes (do not mash berries). Add another cup of sugar and boil 5 minutes. Add the remaining cup of sugar and boil 5 minutes. Pour into glass pie plates and let stand overnight to let the berries absorb as much syrup as possible. The following day, turn into clean, dry jelly glasses or canning jars. Seal (page 8), and process 10 minutes in a Boiling-Water Bath (page 9). *Yield: 3 to 4 eight-ounce glasses.*

Tomato Preserves

Plum or pear tomatoes are those small, thick-fleshed types available toward the end of summer.

1 pound yellow or red plum tomatoes
2 cups sugar
3 or 4 pieces crystallized ginger, finely
  chopped
Grated rind and strained juice of 1 lemon

Drop the tomatoes into rapidly boiling water for one minute. Transfer to cold water and quickly peel off the skins. Cover the tomatoes with the sugar in a bowl and let stand overnight.

The following day, drain the syrup into a kettle and boil until clear and thick. Skim the foam, then add the ginger, lemon rind and juice, and tomatoes; cook until the fruit is clear, about 20 to 30 minutes. Pour into clean, dry jelly glasses or pint canning jars. Seal (page 8), and process 10 minutes in a Boiling-Water Bath (page 9). *Yield: 2 to 2½ eight-ounce glasses.*

Apricot Butter

This is similar to Peach Butter, but has a plain apricot flavor, made tart by lemon juice.

4 to 5 pounds ripe apricots
2 cups water (approximately)
3 cups sugar (approximately)
2 tablespoons strained lemon juice

Remove the stems, cut the apricots in half, and remove the pits; do not peel. Place the apricots in a medium kettle, with water just to cover (use as little water as possible—add just enough to prevent the fruit from scorching until it begins to render its own juices). Simmer the apricots until they are completely soft, 15 to 30 minutes. Force through a sieve or put through a food mill. Measure the pulp; there should be about 3 cups. Add an equal amount of sugar and turn into the kettle. Boil slowly over medium heat, stirring constantly, until thickened, about 30 minutes. Remove from heat, add the lemon juice, stir well, and turn into clean, dry, hot pint canning jars. Seal (page 8), and process 10 minutes in a Boiling-Water Bath (page 9). *Yield: about 4 pints.*

Pear Honey Butter

2 pounds juicy ripe pears (Bartlett are good)
2 cups honey
1 tablespoon strained lemon juice
2 cups cider vinegar
½ teaspoon ground cinnamon
½ teaspoon ground allspice

Peel, quarter, and core the pears. Combine with remaining ingredients in a kettle. Stirring occasionally, simmer over low heat until thick, about 30 to 40 minutes. Pour into clean, dry half-pint canning jars. Seal (page 8), and process 10 minutes in a Boiling-Water Bath (page 9). *Yield: 1 to 1½ pints.*

Spiced Peach Butter

4 pounds ripe peaches
2 cups water
2 to 3 cups sugar (approximately)
2 teaspoons ground cinnamon
½ teaspoon ground allspice
¼ teaspoon ground cloves
1 teaspoon ground nutmeg
½ teaspoon ground ginger

Pit the peaches, but do not peel them. Cut into small pieces and combine with the water in a medium kettle. Over low heat, cook until soft, about 15 to 20 minutes. Force the fruit through a sieve or put through a food mill. Measure the pulp; add 2/3 cup of sugar for each cup of pulp. Combine in the kettle along with the cinnamon, allspice, and cloves and boil rapidly over medium-high heat until the mixture begins to thicken, about 20 to 30 minutes. Add the nutmeg and ginger and continue to boil until the butter mounds on a spoon, about 10 minutes. Turn into clean, dry half-pint canning jars. Seal (page 8), and process 10 minutes in a Boiling-Water Bath (page 9). *Yield: 3 to 4 pints.*

Grape-Apple Butter

5 pounds ripe Concord grapes
5 medium-size tart apples (McIntosh are good)
1 cup water (approximately)
3 cups sugar
1½ teaspoons ground allspice
1 teaspoon ground nutmeg
1 teaspoon ground cinnamon
½ teaspoon ground cloves

Remove the stems from the grapes, mash in a kettle, and simmer until juicy and tender, about 15 to 20 minutes. Remove the stems, blossom ends, and cores of the apples and cut up finely. Add apples to grapes, barely cover fruit with water, and simmer over low heat until soft. Force through a sieve or put through a food mill. Add the sugar and spices and boil rapidly, stirring often, until the butter is thick and mounds on a spoon. Pour into clean, dry half-pint canning jars. Seal (page 8), and process 10 minutes in a Boiling-Water Bath (page 9). *Yield: 2 pints.*

Peach Butter

4 pounds ripe peaches, pitted
2 cups water
2 to 3 cups sugar (approximately)
2 teaspoons ground cinnamon
1 teaspoon ground allspice
¼ teaspoon ground cloves

Cut the unpeeled peaches into small pieces and put in a kettle with the water; simmer over low heat until soft. Force through a sieve or put through a food mill. Measure; add 2/3 cup of sugar for each cup of pulp. Add the spices and boil rapidly, stirring occasionally, until thick enough to mound on a spoon, about 30 minutes. Pour into clean, dry half-pint canning jars. Seal (page 8), and process 10 minutes in a Boiling-Water Bath (page 9). *Yield: 3 to 4 pints.*

Spicy Apple Butter

Old-timers often stored apple and other fruit butters in a crock with a heavy plate for a cover. That was great when there were cold cellars for storage, but most houses don't have them. Today, we use canning jars instead.

4 pounds tart apples (McIntosh are good)
2 cups sweet cider
3 to 4 cups sugar (approximately)
1 tablespoon ground cinnamon
1 teaspoon ground cloves
½ teaspoon ground allspice

Remove the stems, blossom ends, and cores of the unpared apples and cut into small pieces. Combine with the cider in a kettle, cover, and simmer over low heat, stirring occasionally, until very soft. Let cool, then force through a sieve or put through a food mill. Measure; add ½ cup of sugar for each cup of fruit. Return to the kettle and add the spices. Simmer, stirring frequently (this scorches easily), until the mixture is dark and thick, about 2 hours. Pour into clean, dry half-pint canning jars. Seal (page 8), and process 10 minutes in a Boiling-Water Bath (page 9). *Yield: 4 to 5 pints.*

Quince Honey

Quinces are rare in modern gardens, where the flowering quinces are more often grown. In New England and in many other areas, however, quinces become available toward the end of the growing season in large enough quantities for preserving. Preserves made with quinces, which are very tart, need more sugar.

3 large quinces
6 cups sugar
1 cup water
½ teaspoon lemon juice (if quinces are very ripe)

Pare and grate the quinces; set aside. Combine the sugar and water in a medium kettle over low heat and stir until the sugar dissolves. Brush down the sides of the kettle with a pastry brush dipped in cold water to remove any sugar crystals that form. Turn the grated quinces into the kettle and cook gently for 15 to 20 minutes. (If the quinces are dead ripe, add ½ teaspoon lemon juice after the first 10 minutes of cooking.) Pour the mixture into clean, dry half-pint canning jars. Seal (page 8), and process 10 minutes in a Boiling-Water Bath (page 9). *Yield: about 3 pints.*

Fruit Butters

Butters may be made from the pulp left over from making jelly if only one juice extraction was made. Place the pulp in a small kettle, add water barely to cover (about ½ to 1 cup), and boil slowly 3 to 5 minutes. Force through a sieve or put through a food mill. Measure; add 2/3 cup of sugar for each cup of pulp. Add spices of your choice and cook slowly, stirring to prevent scorching, until thick. Pour into clean, dry half-pint canning jars. Seal (page 8), and process 10 minutes in a Boiling-Water Bath (page 9).

Tomato-Apple Butter

Spicier than tomato butter, this includes fresh gingerroot. Use firm, meaty, but really ripe tomatoes, preferably the type called Italian or plum tomatoes, or use the tomatoes that are recommended for canning. Tomatoes that are too juicy will take longer to cook. Use a slow-cooking electric crock pot, if you have one; much less stirring is necessary during the long cooking period at the end.

2½ pounds ripe tomatoes (about 8 to 10 medium)
2 medium-size tart apples
2 cups sugar
1 cup cider vinegar
One 1-inch cinnamon stick, 1 blade of mace, 6 whole cloves, and one 1-inch piece fresh gingerroot, tied in a cloth or cheesecloth bag

Remove the stems and peel the tomatoes (to peel easily, dip them in boiling water for 30 to 60 seconds). Cut into thick pieces. Peel, core, and slice the apples. In a large kettle, combine the tomatoes and apples. Stir in the sugar, vinegar, and the spices. Stir over low heat until the sugar dissolves, then simmer, stirring occasionally, until thickened, about 2 to 3 hours. When the butter is very thick and mounds on a spoon, remove the spice bag and pour into clean, dry half-pint canning jars. Seal (page 8), and process 10 minutes in a Boiling-Water Bath (page 9). *Yield: about 2 to 2½ pints.*

Relishes

Relishes

Relishes delight the eye and tickle the appetite. They perk up plain dishes — pepper relish with meat loaf is a must for both family and company. A relish tray of assorted kinds (corn, beet, and cucumber, for instance) is not only a grace note to almost any dinner but, accompanied by crackers, also enhances the cocktail hour.

Chutneys go with almost any meat dish, and do wondrous things when served with curried chicken, veal, or lamb. The recipe for the famous Major Grey's Mango Chutney was, and is, a closely guarded secret. But we've collected some marvelous chutney recipes from friends and neighbors.

Tomato catsup made in your own kitchen, as well as the unusual green tomato or cranberry catsups, are conversation pieces at picnics and share-the-cooking parties. And you'll find that homemade tomato paste and barbecue sauces are great improvements over the bottled varieties.

EQUIPMENT AND PROCESSING

Most of the equipment needed for making relishes is used in making other preserves; see page 6. Use medium-size kettles.

Many of these recipes call for processing in a Boiling-Water Bath (page 9). For others where Boiling-Water Bath processing is not absolutely necessary, seal jars as indicated on page 8. Use regular canning jars for foods to be processed in a Boiling-Water Bath.

If you live at an altitude higher than 1,000 feet above sea level, see the chart on page 9.

Marcie's Nectarine Chutney

Marcie sometimes substitutes dates for the raisins and peaches for the nectarines.

5 cups sliced, pitted, peeled nectarines
¼ cup finely chopped seeded green pepper
¾ cup seedless raisins
2 cups sugar
1½ cups cider vinegar
½ cup cut-up crystallized ginger
¼ teaspoon salt
¼ teaspoon each whole cloves and all-spice, and two 3-inch cinnamon sticks, tied in a cloth or cheesecloth bag

Combine all the ingredients in a medium kettle, then heat to boiling. Boil until the mixture is dark and syrupy, about 1½ hours. Remove the spice bag. Turn into clean, dry, hot half-pint or pint canning jars. Seal and process 10 minutes in a Boiling-Water Bath (page 9). *Yield: 2 to 2½ pints.*

Marcie's Apricot Chutney

5 cups chopped pitted apricots
2 medium white onions, sliced
1 cup seedless white raisins
Skin and pulp of ½ seeded lemon, chopped
Skin and pulp of ½ seeded orange, chopped
½ sweet green or red pepper, seeded and finely chopped
1½ cups firmly packed brown sugar
1¾ cups cider vinegar
¼ cup finely chopped crystallized ginger
2 tablespoons mustard seed
1 teaspoon salt
½ teaspoon ground mace

Combine all the ingredients in a large kettle and boil slowly, stirring often, until thick, about 1½ hours. Turn into clean, dry, hot half-pint or pint canning jars. Seal, and process 10 minutes in a Boiling-Water Bath (page 9). *Yield: 2 to 2½ pints.*

Idah's Fresh Prune Chutney

Italian prune plums are a variety of plum.

1½ pounds Italian prune plums (about 20)
1 cup firmly packed light brown sugar
1 cup granulated sugar
2 large cloves garlic, thinly sliced
1 small onion, thinly sliced
¾ cup cider vinegar
½ cup finely chopped crystallized ginger
2 teaspoons salt
2 teaspoons mustard seed
1½ teaspoons crushed red pepper

Cut the plums in half, then pit. Combine the remaining ingredients in a kettle, and bring to a boil over medium heat. Add the plums and simmer over low heat about one hour, stirring frequently, until the mixture is thick. Pour into clean, dry, hot half-pint canning jars. Seal, and process 10 minutes in a Boiling-Water Bath (page 9). *Yield: 1½ to 1¾ pints.*

Doris Smith's Cranberry Chutney

2½ cups cranberries
1 cup seedless white raisins
½ cup thinly sliced onion
2 cups cider or apple juice
½ cup cider vinegar
1 cup firmly packed brown sugar
½ lemon, sliced
Strained juice of ½ lemon
6 tablespoons slivered crystallized ginger
1 teaspoon chili powder
1 teaspoon dry mustard
½ teaspoon salt

Combine all the ingredients in a large kettle. Stirring frequently to prevent scorching, simmer over low heat 20 to 25 minutes or until the mixture is thick and the cranberries are tender. Turn into clean, dry jelly glasses or canning jars. Seal, and process 10 minutes in a Boiling-Water Bath (page 9). *Yield: 4 to 5 eight-ounce glasses.*

Clovelly Chutney

6 large firm pears (Seckel are good)
One 15-ounce package seedless raisins
3 cups cider vinegar
2 cups firmly packed dark brown sugar
5 pieces crystallized ginger, finely chopped
4 cloves garlic, finely chopped
2 tablespoons mustard seed
1 tablespoon salt
Few grains cayenne pepper

Peel the pears; remove cores and seeds. Cut the fruit into small pieces and combine with remaining ingredients in a kettle. Boil over medium heat, stirring frequently to prevent scorching, until very thick. Pour into clean, dry jelly glasses or canning jars. Seal, and process 10 minutes in a Boiling-Water Bath (page 9). *Yield: 6 eight-ounce jars.*

Clovelly Apple Chutney

Substitute 6 large firm apples for the pears in Clovelly Chutney (above). Increase the brown sugar to 2½ cups, and proceed with the recipe.

Kiwi Chutney

Kiwis are a tropical fruit, small and oval in shape, with fuzzy brown skins. Fruit and vegetable specialty shops carry them seasonally. The pulp is bright green with many tiny seeds. The taste is sweet-tart.

To make Kiwi Chutney, substitute 12 to 14 kiwis for the pears in Clovelly Chutney (above) and proceed with the recipe.

Corn Relish

In New England, this is often served with crackers as a cocktail spread.

4 or 5 medium ears corn, husked
2 green peppers, seeded and diced
2 sweet red peppers, seeded and diced
1 large or 2 small onions, coarsely chopped
1 cup chopped celery
½ cup sugar
2 cups cider vinegar
½ tablespoon salt
½ teaspoon celery seed
½ tablespoon dry mustard
¼ teaspoon turmeric

Put the corn in boiling water to cover and cook 5 minutes. Remove, plunge into cold water, then drain. With a sharp knife pressed against the husk, cut off the kernels. Set aside.

In a medium kettle, combine the peppers, onion, celery, sugar, vinegar, salt, and celery seed. Boil 5 minutes, stirring occasionally. In a cup, mix the mustard and turmeric with a little of the boiling liquid and add the mixture to the kettle. Add the corn kernels and boil slowly 5 minutes over medium heat, stirring occasionally. Pack into clean, dry half-pint or pint canning jars. Seal, and process 15 minutes in a Boiling-Water Bath (page 9). *Yield: about 1½ pints.*

All-Time Favorite Pepper Relish

6 green peppers
6 sweet red peppers
2 medium or 1 large Spanish onion, cut up
8 cups boiling water
1 cup sugar
½ teaspoon salt
1 cup cider vinegar

Remove the seeds and membranes from the peppers. Put the peppers and onions through a food chopper, using a medium blade. Put in a kettle and pour the boiling water over the vegetables. Let stand 10 minutes. Drain, then add the remaining ingredients and boil, stirring occasionally, about 20 minutes. Pour into clean, dry half-pint or pint canning jars. Seal, and process 10 minutes in a Boiling-Water Bath (page 9). *Yield: about 1 pint.*

Vegetable-Garden Relish

4 pounds ripe tomatoes (12 to 14 medium)
2 cups diced celery
2 cups diced onions
3 sweet red or green peppers, seeded and diced
2 cups canned tomato juice
1 tablespoon sugar
1½ tablespoons salt
¼ teaspoon pepper

Remove the stems and peel the tomatoes (to peel easily, dip them in boiling water for 30 to 60 seconds). Cut into quarters and set aside. Combine the celery, onions, peppers, and tomato juice in a medium kettle. Simmer over medium heat 20 minutes. Add the tomatoes, sugar, salt, and pepper. Bring to a boil. Boil rapidly one minute (no less), then pack into pint canning jars. Fill the jars with the pickling liquid to within ¼ inch of the rims. Seal, and process 30 minutes in a Boiling-Water Bath (page 9). *Yield: about 5 to 6 pints.*

Horseradish Relish

Plant a few horseradish seeds in an out-of-the-way corner of the garden. The roots spread rapidly, so don't plant near landscaped areas. The seeds may also be planted in a container garden. Use the full-grown roots for your own zesty relish — they're much sharper and better than the commercial products.

1 cup grated or cubed peeled fresh horseradish
½ cup white vinegar
¼ teaspoon salt

Put the horseradish through a food chopper, using a fine blade, or grind in a blender. Mix with the remaining ingredients. Pack into clean, dry jars and cap tightly. Store in the refrigerator. *Yield: 2 to 3 four-ounce jars.*

Beet Relish

2 cups ground or finely chopped cooked
   beets
2 cups ground or finely chopped cabbage
¼ cup prepared horseradish
½ cup sugar
1½ teaspoons salt
1½ to 2 cups cider vinegar

Combine beets, cabbage, horseradish, sugar, and salt in an earthenware or glass bowl. Mix well, then pack into clean, dry half-pint or pint canning jars. Bring the vinegar to a boil and pour over the mixture in the jars. Seal, and process 15 minutes in a Boiling-Water Bath (page 9). *Yield: about 2 pints.*

Waste-Not Want-Not Celery Relish

This is Thalia's way of using up the coarse outer stalks of celery, an excellent relish made from what often gets thrown away.

1 quart chopped celery
1 cup chopped white onions
1 quart water
1 tablespoon salt
2 large green peppers, seeded and chopped
3 large sweet red peppers, seeded and
   chopped
2 cups vinegar
½ cup sugar
1 teaspoon salt
1 teaspoon dry mustard

Put the celery and the onions into 2 separate small kettles. Combine the water and the tablespoon of salt and divide between the kettles, covering the ingredients in each container. (If you haven't enough brine, mix more in the proportion of ¼ teaspoon of salt to 1 cup of water.) Boil the celery and onions 10 minutes. Drain well. Place the remaining ingredients in a medium kettle, add the celery and onions, and bring to a boil over medium heat. Reduce the heat and simmer until the vegetables are tender, about 30 to 40 minutes. Pack into clean, dry half-pint canning jars. Seal, and process 10 minutes in a Boiling-Water Bath (page 9). *Yield: about 3 to 3½ pints.*

Harriet's Tomato Catsup

5 pounds ripe tomatoes (about 20 medium)
2 medium onions, sliced
2 green peppers, seeded and cut into strips

For every 2 quarts vegetable pulp:
1 cup cider vinegar
¼ cup sugar
1 tablespoon salt
1 teaspoon celery salt
1 teaspoon dry mustard
1 teaspoon paprika
1 teaspoon each whole allspice and cloves,
   and 1 cinnamon stick, tied in a cloth or
   cheesecloth bag

Cut off and discard any green unripened parts of the tomatoes. Cut the tomatoes into chunks and combine in a kettle with the onions and peppers. Simmer until the vegetables are soft, about 10 to 15 minutes. Force through a sieve and return to the kettle. The pulp will be watery; reduce over medium-high heat by about a fourth.

Measure the pulp; for every 2 quarts, add the vinegar, sugar, and seasonings as listed in the ingredients column. Stirring often, boil slowly to thicken the mixture, about 40 to 60 minutes. Remove the spice bag. Pour the catsup into clean, dry half-pint or pint canning jars. Seal, and process 10 minutes in a Boiling-Water Bath (page 9). *Yield: 2 pints.*

Green Tomato Catsup

4 pounds green tomatoes (16 to 18 small)
2 medium onions
1/3 cup pickling or kosher salt (approximately)
8 cups water (approximately)
1 cup firmly packed brown sugar
½ cup cider vinegar
1 tablespoon prepared mustard
2 tablespoons whole mixed pickling spices
   (optional)
1 teaspoon salt
½ teaspoon black peppercorns
½ teaspoon each ground allspice, cinnamon, and ginger

Slice the tomatoes and the onions. Layer in a large earthenware or glass bowl. Dissolve the 1/3 cup of salt in the water; barely cover the vegetables with the brine. Let stand overnight.

The following day, drain the vegetables and put in a large kettle with the remaining ingredients. Stirring occasionally, boil slowly over medium heat until thick, about 1½ to 2 hours. Force through a sieve and pour into clean, dry half-pint or pint canning jars. Seal, and process 10 minutes in a Boiling-Water Bath (page 9). *Yield: about 2 pints.*

Celery Catsup

A delicious variation of tomato catsup. Use meaty tomatoes to make this.

12 large ripe tomatoes
2 large stalks celery
4 large onions, sliced
1 sweet red pepper, seeded and cut up
½ pound firmly packed light brown sugar
1 cup cider vinegar
1 tablespoon salt

Remove the stems and peel the tomatoes (to peel easily, dip them in boiling water for 30 to 60 seconds). Chop the tomatoes, celery, onions, and pepper in the blender, a little at a time, until they are finely chopped. Combine with the remaining ingredients in a medium kettle. Stir over low heat until the sugar dissolves. Raise the heat to medium-low and boil slowly, stirring occasionally, about 1½ hours. Pour into clean, dry half-pint canning jars. Seal, and process 10 minutes in a Boiling-Water Bath (page 9). *Yield: about 2½ to 3 pints.*

Cranberry Catsup

2 pounds cranberries
2 medium onions
1 cup water
2 cups sugar
1 cup cider vinegar
1½ teaspoons each ground cloves, cinnamon, allspice, and pepper
½ teaspoon salt

Combine the cranberries, onions, and water in a kettle. Boil slowly over medium-low heat until tender, about 10 to 20 minutes, then force through a sieve. Add the remaining ingredients and boil, stirring often, until thick, about 1 to 1½ hours. Pour into clean, dry half-pint or pint canning jars. Seal, and process 10 minutes in a Boiling-Water Bath (Page 9). *Yield: 1 to 1½ pints.*

Italian Tomato Paste

If Italian cooking is popular in your home, then make small batches of tomato paste at the peak of the tomato season. It is a great luxury. Use meaty Italian tomatoes. If you have a slow-cooking electric crock pot, use it for the long cooking period at the end.

4 pounds ripe tomatoes (about 12 to 14 medium or 18 to 24 small)
1 medium carrot, scraped and diced
1 medium white onion, diced
¼ cup chopped celery
1 tablespoon minced fresh basil
1 teaspoon salt
1 half-inch piece stick cinnamon and ½ teaspoon each whole black peppercorns and cloves, tied in a cheesecloth bag

Remove the stems of the tomatoes and slice thinly. Combine in a medium kettle with the remaining ingredients. Simmer over medium heat, stirring occasionally, until very soft, about 20 to 30 minutes. Remove the spice bag. Force the mixture through a sieve or put through a food mill; return spice bag to mixture. In a double boiler, over boiling water, simmer until very thick, about 2½ to 3 hours. Remove the spice bag. Pour the mixture into clean, dry 6-ounce canning jars. Seal, and process 5 minutes in a Boiling-Water Bath (page 9). *Yield: 2 to 3 six-ounce jars.*

Spiced Vinegar

1 quart cider vinegar
1 tablespoon whole mixed pickling spices
2 tablespoons whole black peppercorns
½ teaspoon ground ginger
⅛ teaspoon cayenne pepper

Combine all the ingredients in a kettle and boil rapidly 15 minutes. Strain through several layers of wet cheesecloth. Pour the vinegar into 16-ounce bottles and seal. *Yield: 2 pints.*

Hot Tomato and Pepper Sauce

This is a really hot sauce, great with grilled meats, red beans, and southwestern or Texas dishes. Wear gloves when working with the hot peppers, and don't touch your face or your eyes. To peel the tomatoes easily, plunge them into a kettleful of boiling water for 30 to 60 seconds, then chill under cold running water a few seconds.

4 packed cups peeled, sliced, ripe tomatoes (about 6 large)
¾ cup seeded, chopped hot red peppers
4 cups vinegar
½ cup sugar
1½ teaspoons salt
1 tablespoon whole mixed pickling spices, tied in a cloth or cheesecloth bag

Combine the tomatoes, hot peppers, and 2 cups of the vinegar in a large kettle. Boil slowly over medium heat until the tomatoes are soft, about 20 minutes. Force the mixture through a sieve or put through a food mill and return to the kettle. Add the sugar, salt, and spice bag. Boil slowly over medium heat, stirring, until the sugar dissolves and the mixture thickens, about 30 minutes. Add the remaining 2 cups of vinegar and continue to cook until thickened, about 20 to 30 minutes. Pour into clean, dry, hot half-pint canning jars, filling them to within ¼ inch of the rims. Seal, and process 15 minutes in a Boiling-Water Bath (page 9). *Yield: about 1 pint.*

Spicy Bar-B-Cue Sauce

The best time to make this sauce is when tomatoes and green peppers are plentiful, toward the end of summer. Use ripe, meaty tomatoes. Wear gloves when handling the hot peppers, and don't touch your face or eyes. Before barbecuing, mix ½ cup of salad oil with each cup of sauce.

4 quarts ripe tomatoes
2 medium onions, cut into quarters
2 cups chopped celery
1½ cups seeded, chopped green or sweet red peppers (about 3 medium)
2 hot red peppers, seeded
1 cup firmly packed light brown sugar
1 cup cider vinegar
2 cloves garlic, crushed
1 teaspoon whole black peppercorns, tied in a small cloth or cheesecloth bag
⅛ teaspoon cayenne pepper
1 tablespoon salt
1 tablespoon powdered mustard
1 tablespoon paprika
1 teaspoon Tabasco sauce

Remove the stems, then scald, peel, and quarter the tomatoes. Combine in a large kettle with the onions, celery, and sweet and hot peppers. Boil slowly over medium heat, stirring occasionally, until the vegetables are soft, about 30 minutes. Put through a food mill (preferably) or force through a sieve. Return the mixture to the kettle and boil slowly over medium heat until reduced by about half, about 45 minutes. Add the remaining ingredients and simmer about 1½ hours over medium-low heat, stirring often, until the mixture has the consistency of catsup. Remove the peppercorns and pour the mixture into clean, dry half-pint canning jars. Seal, and process 20 minutes in a Boiling-Water Bath (page 9). *Yield: 2 to 2½ pints.*

Pickles

Pickles

Pickling is one of the oldest preserving methods we know, and its roots are deeply embedded in American pioneer traditions. The early settlers relied on pickling to put by much of their winter supplies, and they pickled almost everything that came to hand, including wild nuts.

Cucumbers are probably the most popular vegetable for pickling. Plump, juicy dill pickles and those delicious sweet-sour bread-and-butter pickle slices are so much in demand by most families that they are well worth making yourself. But there are lots of other vegetables you will find pleasure in pickling. Baby beets, carrots, even zucchini can make good pickles, while artichoke hearts and mushrooms make very elegant pickles indeed. You can even pickle nasturtium seeds and call them capers, a luxury item harder and harder to find and wonderful combined with all sorts of meats and sauces.

Most of the recipes in this chapter are for fresh-pack, or quick-process, pickles and are easy to prepare. These call for a short period of brining; that is, the vegetables are soaked in salted water a few hours or overnight. After draining they are combined with vinegar, spices, and other seasonings and processed in a Boiling-Water Bath (page 9). They lend themselves to preparation in mini-batches.

Fruits and vegetables for pickling must be fresh, unblemished, and perfectly clean. Slavishly observe the following rules:

☐ Choose fresh, firm, young vegetables and fruits and use them as soon as possible after picking or buying. If you cannot use them at once, keep in the refrigerator until pickling time. Discard any vegetables or fruits that have even the slightest sign of mold. This will produce an off-flavor.

☐ Use unwaxed cucumbers for pickling whole, since brine cannot penetrate a waxed surface. If the only available cucumbers are waxed, quickly dip them two or three times in boiling water, then wipe with paper towels to remove the wax.

☐ Wash all vegetables and fruits thoroughly in cold water. Use a brush to remove all clinging soil. Lift the vegetables from the water instead of pouring off the water.

☐ Use pure granulated pickling salt if you can get it. Kosher salt is good and is generally available. Ordinary table salt contains material to prevent caking, which will make the brine cloudy. Iodized salt will darken pickles. One-third cup of salt for each quart of water makes a pickling brine—what old-timers say should be "strong enough to float an egg."

☐ Use a good grade of commercial distilled white or cider vinegar. It has 4 to 6% acidity, which the pickles need for preservation; homemade vinegars may not be acetic enough.

☐ Use granulated or light- or dark-brown sugar. If using brown sugar, pack the measuring cup tightly. Brown sugar darkens the pickles slightly.

☐ Make sure that your spices are very fresh (see page 10).

EQUIPMENT

Use unchipped enamelware, stainless steel, aluminum, or glass utensils for heating pickling liquids. *Do not* use copper, brass, galvanized, or iron utensils. These metals react with acids and salts, cause unappetizing color changes in the pickles, and can create undesirable compounds.

For overnight salting, use a crock or stone jar, an earthenware or glass bowl, or a large casserole. Use a plate or a glass lid that fits inside the container to cover the vegetables in the brine. We often fill a glass jar with water to weight the cover so that the vegetables will stay under the brine. Protect marinating ingredients by covering the container with a large, clean towel.

Additionally, you will need:

☐ A vegetable peeler

☐ Sharp knives

☐ A wooden cutting board

☐ A measuring cup

☐ A measuring spoon

☐ A large tablespoon

☐ A colander

☐ A food chopper or grinder, or a blender

☐ Canning jars and lids

☐ A large kettle for the Boiling-Water Bath process

PROCESSING

Although vinegar and brine are preservatives, we recommend preserving pickles by the Boiling-Water Bath (page 9). There is always the danger that organisms that cause spoilage will enter the food when it is transferred from kettle to jar, no matter how careful you are. Sealing instructions are discussed on page 8.

If you live at an altitude higher than 1,000 feet above sea level, add one minute to the processing time for each additional 1,000 feet (see chart on page 9).

Sweet Gherkins

2 quarts pickling cucumbers (about 3
   pounds)
2½ cups water
½ cup pickling or kosher salt
2 quarts cider vinegar
4 cups sugar
2 tablespoons whole allspice
1 tablespoon celery seed
½ cup mustard seed
One 3-inch cinnamon stick and 2 tablespoons whole cloves, tied in a cloth or
   cheesecloth bag

The stem ends of the unpeeled cucumbers
may be left on. Place them in a 3- to 5-quart
crock. In a kettle, bring the water and the
salt to a boil and pour over the cucumbers.
(The brine should cover the cucumbers; if
necessary, make more.) Cover and let stand
24 hours. Drain.

Bring the vinegar to a boil and pour over
the cucumbers. Cover and let stand 24
hours. Drain, reserving the vinegar. Add
the sugar and the spices to the vinegar. Boil
the mixture rapidly 5 minutes; remove the
spice bag. Pack the cucumbers into clean,
dry, hot half-pint or pint canning jars to
within ½ inch of the rims. Add boiling
syrup to cover, filling to within ¼ inch of
the rims. Seal, and process 5 minutes in a
Boiling-Water Bath (page 9). *Yield: 3 to 4
pints.*

Never-Fail Dill Pickles

20 pickling cucumbers
2 large sprigs dill
2 medium cloves garlic
1½ cups water
½ cup distilled white vinegar
1 tablespoon pickling or kosher salt

Slice the unpeeled cucumbers lengthwise
into halves. Fill 2 clean, dry, hot pint canning jars with the cucumbers and tuck a
sprig of dill and a clove of garlic, split in
half, into each jar. Mix the water, vinegar,
and salt and bring to a rapid boil. Pour into
the jars, filling to within ¼ inch of the rims.
Seal, and process 5 minutes in a Boiling-
Water Bath (page 9). *Yield: 2 pints.*

Doris Smith's Emergency Dill Pickles

Doris worked out this recipe to provide
herself with sweet dill pickles when her
garden — and the greengrocer's shelves —
had no fresh pickling cucumbers to offer.
It's the easiest way to pickle, if not the most
authentic, and the results are delicious.

2 quarts commercial whole dill pickles
1½ cups sugar
1½ cups cider vinegar
2 tablespoons vegetable oil
2 medium cloves garlic, minced
2 tablespoons whole black peppercorns
2 tablespoons whole allspice

Cut the drained pickles into ¾-inch-thick
slices. Place the slices in clean, dry, hot
half-pint canning jars, filling to within ½
inch of the rims. Combine the sugar, vinegar, oil, garlic, peppercorns, and allspice in
a medium kettle. Bring to a rapid boil over
high heat. Pour into the jars, filling to
within ¼ inch of the rims. Seal, and process 5 minutes in a Boiling-Water Bath
(page 9). *Yield: about 1 pint.*

Cross-Cut Pickles

The best cucumbers to use for this recipe are the types usually sold under the name of Burpless Hybrid. Large and on the long side, they are especially mild cucumbers. If you are growing your own cucumbers to pickle, you will find burpless types offered in the seed catalogs with names such as Tastygreen and Sweet Slice Hybrid.

3 pounds cucumbers, diagonally sliced
3 medium onions, sliced
1 very large clove garlic
3 tablespoons pickling or kosher salt
About 18 ice cubes (1 tray)
2¼ cups sugar
1½ cups white vinegar
1 tablespoon mustard seed
¾ teaspoon turmeric
¾ teaspoon celery seed

Toss the unpeeled cucumbers with onions in a large bowl until mixed well. Peel the garlic clove (and it should be a really big one) and place it in the bowl. Toss the cucumbers and the onions with the garlic, stopping occasionally to sprinkle with some of the salt. When you have used up the salt, and the cucumbers, onions, garlic, and salt are thoroughly mixed, cover with ice cubes and let stand at least 3 hours— but preferably 5 to 6—at room temperature.

Drain the cucumber liquid that has accumulated in the bowl and remove the garlic clove. In a large kettle, combine the sugar, vinegar, mustard seed, turmeric, and celery seed. Bring just to a boil over medium-high heat and immediately add the drained cucumbers and onions. Heat 5 minutes without allowing the liquid to boil. Pack the vegetables into clean, dry, hot half-pint canning jars, filling to within ½ inch of the rims. Pour in the pickling liquid, filling to within ¼ inch of the rims. Seal, and process 5 minutes in a Boiling-Water Bath (page 9). *Yield: 2 to 2½ pints.*

Bread-and-Butter Pickles

These are our children's favorites, mild pickles that are delicious with—bread and butter.

12 small to medium pickling cucumbers
3 medium onions, very thinly sliced
¼ cup plus 2 tablespoons pickling or
    kosher salt
2 cups sugar
2 cups distilled white vinegar
1 cup water
1½ tablespoons celery seed
1½ tablespoons mustard seed
½ teaspoon ground allspice

Cut the unpeeled cucumbers into ¼-inch-thick rounds; measure 12 cups. Parboil 2 minutes in rapidly boiling water; drain at once and plunge into cool water. Drain and let dry. Layer the cucumber and onion slices in a large bowl, sprinkling each cucumber layer with some of the salt. Cover and let stand 12 hours.

Drain the vegetables and rinse in cool water. In a large kettle, combine the sugar, vinegar, water, celery seed, mustard seed, and allspice. Stir over medium heat until the sugar dissolves, then raise the heat and boil 3 minutes. Add the cucumber and onion slices to the syrup and return just to a boil. Pack the vegetables at once into clean, dry, hot half-pint or pint canning jars, filling to within ½ inch of the rims. Add boiling syrup to cover, filling to within ¼ inch of the rims. Seal, and process 5 minutes in a Boiling-Water Bath (page 9). *Yield: 4 pints.*

Mary Pearl's Maple Sugar Pickles

New Englanders made these pickles in a stone crock in late summer, storing them in a cool shed or cellar for fall and winter use. The brine used here is strong. If you need more than the 2 quarts of brine called for, mix it in the proportion of 1/3 cup of salt to 2 quarts of water.

5 or 6 salad cucumbers, each 6 to 7 inches long
2 quarts water (approximately)
1/3 cup pickling or kosher salt (approximately)
1½ pounds maple sugar
2 cups cider vinegar
1½ teaspoons ground cinnamon
½ teaspoon ground allspice
½ teaspoon ground cloves

Peel the cucumbers and cut lengthwise into quarters. Place in a large crock or bowl. Mix the water with the salt and pour over the cucumbers just to cover. Cover and let stand overnight.

The following day, drain the cucumbers. In a medium kettle, combine the maple sugar, vinegar, and spices. Add the cucumbers and boil slowly until tender, about 30 minutes. Pack the cucumber quarters into clean, dry, hot pint canning jars, filling to within ½ inch of the rims. Add boiling syrup to cover, filling to within ¼ inch of the rims. Seal, and process 5 minutes in a Boiling-Water Bath (page 9). *Yield: 5 pints.*

Cucumber Rings

4 salad cucumbers, each 6 to 7 inches long
½ cup pickling or kosher salt
2 medium onions
½ green pepper, seeded
½ sweet red pepper, seeded
1½ cups sugar
1½ cups distilled white vinegar
1½ teaspoons mustard seed
½ teaspoon celery seed
½ teaspoon turmeric

Cut the unpeeled cucumbers into ⅛-inch-thick rounds and measure 9 cups. Put into a large earthenware or glass bowl and sprinkle each layer with some of the salt. Cover and let stand overnight (or at least 4 hours), then drain thoroughly.

Slice the onions ⅛ inch thick and coarsely chop the peppers; mix with the remaining ingredients. Put in a medium kettle with the cucumber slices and bring just to a boil. Pour into clean, dry, hot pint canning jars. Seal, and process 5 minutes in a Boiling-Water Bath (page 9). *Yield: 4 pints.*

Too-Many-Cucumbers Pickle

1 quart cider vinegar
¼ cup sugar
¼ cup salt
¼ cup dry mustard
1½ quarts small cucumbers (1½ to 2½ inches long)

Combine vinegar, sugar, salt, and mustard, mixing well. Divide among 3 clean, dry pint jars and cover. As small cucumbers become available, cut them from the vine, leaving ¼ inch of stem on the cucumbers. Rinse and dry very carefully, and pack each day's crop into the vinegar mixture. When all the jars are filled, seal, and store in a cool place 2 months before using. *Yield: 3 pints.*

Zucchini Pickles

2 pounds 6-inch zucchini (5 or 6)
½ cup pickling or kosher salt
½ cup sugar
1½ cups distilled white vinegar
3 tablespoons dry mustard
1 tablespoon ground ginger
1 tablespoon curry powder
6 whole black peppercorns

Cut the unpeeled zucchini into ½-inch-thick rounds. Put in a large earthenware or glass bowl, sprinkling each layer with some of the salt. Let stand overnight.

The following day, drain the squash, rinse in cold water, and place in a large kettle. Combine the sugar, vinegar, and spices in a saucepan and boil 5 minutes. Pour the boiling syrup over the squash. Bring the squash to a boil and simmer 5 minutes or until tender but not mushy. Spoon the mixture into clean, dry, hot pint canning jars, filling to within ¼ inch of the rims. Seal, and process 5 minutes in a Boiling-Water Bath (page 9). *Yield: 6 pints.*

Pickled Nasturtium Seeds (Capers)

The edible nasturtiums are *Tropaeolum majus*, the common garden variety.

2 cups nasturtium seeds
2 whole cloves
1 blade of mace or ⅛ teaspoon ground
  mace
2 cups white wine vinegar
½ teaspoon salt

Put the nasturtium seeds, cloves, and mace in a small crock or jar. Heat the vinegar and salt just to a boil and pour over the seeds. Tightly cover the crock or jar and let stand one month. Pack the seeds into small jars and cover with the pickling liquid, filling to within ¼ inch of the rims. Cover with lids. *Yield: about 1½ pints.*

Pickled Sweet Red Peppers

2½ pounds sweet red peppers (5 or 6 large),
  seeded
2 cups sugar
2 cups tarragon vinegar
2 cups water
½ teaspoon celery seed
½ teaspoon mustard seed
2 cloves garlic, crushed
1 teaspoon pickling or kosher salt

Cut the peppers into thin strips. Drop into boiling water to cover, return the water to a boil, and boil, covered, over high heat 3 minutes. Drain.

Combine the remaining ingredients in a large kettle, bring to a boil, and simmer 5 minutes over low heat. Pack the hot peppers into clean, dry, hot pint canning jars, filling to within ½ inch of the rims. Pour the boiling pickling liquid into the jars, filling to within ¼ inch of the rims. Seal, and process 10 minutes in a Boiling-Water Bath (page 9). *Yield: 4 pints.*

Pickled Beets

When you have lots of beets coming up in the vegetable garden and it's time to thin the rows, turn the baby beets into this delicious pickle. Pickled beets make excellent garnishes for pork dishes as well as other meats, and are great in cool summer salads.

24 to 30 small beets (2 to 3 inches in diameter)
2 cups cider vinegar
¾ cup sugar
One 2-inch cinnamon stick and ½ teaspoon whole cloves, tied in a cloth or cheesecloth bag

Cut away the tops of the beets, leaving about 2 inches of stem. Place in a large kettle of cold water, cover, and boil rapidly over high heat until tender, about 15 to 30 minutes (depending on the freshness of the beets). To test doneness, remove one beet from the kettle, run cold water over it, then remove the stem end. Holding the beet by the root tip, squeeze it in a way that will pull on the skin; if the beet is done, the skin will simply slip off. When the beets have cooled, drain and turn into a large bowl of cold water. Slip off the skins. Cut the beets into thin slices. (There should be about 4 cups.)

Combine the remaining ingredients in a medium kettle and simmer 10 minutes over medium heat. Add the beet slices and simmer 10 minutes longer. Pack the beets into clean, dry half-pint canning jars, filling to within ½ inch of the rims. Pour the pickling liquid over the beets, filling to within ¼ inch of the rims. Seal, and process 10 minutes in a Boiling-Water Bath (page 9). *Yield: about 1 pint.*

Pickled Onions

Peeling the onions for this recipe is a chore, but the end product has many interesting uses — in salads, on a relish tray, as a garnish for cold cuts. The smaller the onion, the more attractive the pickle.

4 cups small white onions
4 quarts water
3 cups salt
15 to 20 whole black peppercorns
6 to 8 whole cloves
3 or 4 large bay leaves
12 to 16 half-inch-wide strips canned pimiento
¼ cup sugar
4 cups vinegar

Drop the onions into boiling water and let stand 2 minutes. Drain and plunge into cold water, then slip off the skins. Place in a 3- or 4-quart crock. Mix the 4 quarts water and the salt, making a brine, and pour over the onions to cover, reserving the remainder. Cover the crock and allow the onions to stand at room temperature for 48 hours. Drain and cover again with brine (mix more, if necessary, in the proportion of ¾ cup of salt to 1 quart of water). Let stand 2 days longer.

After 2 days, mix enough brine in a large kettle to cover the onions. Bring to a rapid boil, add the drained onions, and boil 3 minutes. Pack the onions into clean, dry half-pint canning jars, filling to within ½ inch of the rims. In each jar place 5 peppercorns, 2 cloves, 1 bay leaf, and 4 pimiento strips. Combine the sugar and vinegar in a saucepan and bring to a boil. Pour the syrup into the jars to within ¼ inch of the rims. Seal, and process 10 minutes in a Boiling-Water Bath (page 9). *Yield: about 1½ to 2 pints.*

Pickled Onion Rings

1½ pounds medium-size yellow onions
Salted water
1 cup sugar
1½ cups cider vinegar
¾ cup water
3 whole cloves
3 whole black peppercorns
2 bay leaves
1 half-inch piece fresh gingerroot or ¼ tea-
    spoon ground ginger
1½ teaspoons pickling or kosher salt
¼ teaspoon cardamom seed

Slice the onions thinly and put in a kettle.
Add salted water to cover; remove onion
slices and boil the water 2 minutes. Pour
the boiling water over the onions in a bowl
and let stand 45 minutes. Rinse the onions
thoroughly under cold running water and
put in a large kettle. Combine the remaining ingredients in a small kettle over low
heat and bring to a boil, stirring until the
sugar dissolves. Boil 5 minutes. Pour the
syrup over the onion rings. Pack the mixture into clean, dry, hot pint canning jars,
adding enough liquid to fill the jars to
within ¼ inch of the rims. Seal, and process 10 minutes in a Boiling-Water Bath
(page 9). *Yield: 2 pints.*

Pickled Mushrooms and Onions

1 pound whole small mushrooms
2 medium onions, thinly sliced
    and separated into rings (1 cup)
1½ cups red wine vinegar
1½ cups water
½ cup firmly packed brown sugar
4 teaspoons pickling or kosher salt
1 teaspoon dried tarragon, crushed
    (optional)

Trim the stem tips of the mushrooms. Combine the remaining ingredients in a
medium kettle and bring the mixture to a
boil. Add the mushrooms. Reduce the heat
and simmer, uncovered, 5 minutes. Lift the
mushrooms and onion rings from the liquid with a slotted spoon; reserve the liquid
and keep hot. Pack the vegetables into
clean, dry, hot half-pint or pint canning
jars, filling to within ½ inch of the rims.
Pour the boiling pickling liquid into the
jars, filling to within ¼ inch of the rims.
Seal, and process 5 minutes in a Boiling-
Water Bath (page 9). *Yield: 2 pints.*

Pickled Artichoke Hearts

4 pounds small artichokes (15 or 16)
4 cups distilled white vinegar
2 quarts water (approximately)
1 cup white wine vinegar
1 clove garlic, crushed
1 tablespoon pickling or kosher salt

Cut the stems off the artichokes. Slice ½ inch off the tops. Pull off all the tough outer leaves. Combine the distilled white vinegar and 4 cups of the water and bring to a boil; add the artichokes. Cover and simmer until a leaf pulls off easily, about 10 minutes. Drain. Cut the artichokes lengthwise into halves. Remove the hairy choke; discard.

Combine the remaining 4 cups of water, the wine vinegar, garlic, and salt in a saucepan and bring to a boil. Pack the artichoke hearts into clean, dry, hot pint canning jars and pour the boiling vinegar mixture over them, filling to within ¼ inch of the rims. Seal, and process 15 minutes in a Boiling-Water Bath (page 9). *Yield: 6 pints.*

Pickled Spiced Celery

1 quart 3-inch pieces celery
1 small green or sweet red pepper, seeded and thinly sliced
1 quart water
1 tablespoon salt
2 cups vinegar
¾ cup sugar
One 1-inch piece stick cinnamon and ½ teaspoon each whole allspice and cloves, tied in a cloth or cheesecloth bag

Combine the celery, pepper slices, water, and salt in a small kettle and simmer until celery is tender, about 30 minutes. Drain.

Combine the remaining ingredients in another kettle and bring to a boil. Boil 3 minutes. Add the vegetables, reduce the heat, and simmer 5 minutes. Remove the spice bag and pack into clean, dry half-pint canning jars. Seal; process 10 minutes in a Boiling-Water Bath (page 9). *Yield: 2 pints.*

Pickled Midget Sweet Corn

16 to 18 ears midget corn
2 cups distilled white vinegar
¾ cup sugar
½ teaspoon whole cloves and ¼ teaspoon whole allspice, tied in a cheesecloth bag

Strip the husks from the little ears and drop the corn into a large kettle of boiling water. Cook 3 minutes, then drain at once. Combine the remaining ingredients in a medium kettle and bring to a rapid boil over high heat. Boil 5 minutes, then drop the blanched corn ears into the pickling liquid and boil rapidly 5 minutes longer. Pack with the pointed tips up into clean, dry, hot half-pint canning jars. Pour the boiling pickling liquid over the ears, filling to within ¼ inch of the rims. Seal, and process 10 minutes in a Boiling-Water Bath (page 9). *Yield: about 1 pint.*

Sweet Pickled Carrots

3 pounds carrots (18 medium)
2 cups boiling water (approximately)
1½ cups sugar
1½ cups cider vinegar
1½ cups water
2 teaspoons mustard seed
3 whole cloves
One 3-inch cinnamon stick

Peel the carrots and cut lengthwise into quarters. Place in a kettle containing the boiling water and boil rapidly until just tender. Drain and reserve.

Combine the remaining ingredients in a small kettle, bring to a boil, reduce the heat, and simmer 20 minutes. Pack the carrots into clean, dry, pint canning jars, filling to within ½ inch of the rims. Add boiling syrup to cover, filling to within ¼ inch of the rims. Seal; process 5 minutes in a Boiling-Water Bath (page 9). *Yield: 3 pints.*

Pickled Dill Beans

2 pounds green beans
1 cup boiling water
3 cups water
1 cup distilled white vinegar
2 cloves garlic, crushed
2 tablespoons pickling or kosher salt
2 teaspoons dill weed
¼ teaspoon cayenne pepper

Trim the ends of the beans and cut into lengths that will fit pint jars. Place the beans in a kettle, pour the boiling water over them, and boil slowly over medium-high heat 3 minutes. Drain. Pack lengthwise into clean, dry, hot pint canning jars. Combine the remaining ingredients in a small kettle and bring to a boil. Pour at once over the beans, covering completely and filling the jars to within ¼ inch of the rims. Seal, and process 10 minutes in a Boiling-Water Bath (page 9). *Yield: 4 pints.*

Pottsfield Pickles

Frank Ball claimed that of all the pickles in the world, Pottsfield Pickles were best. We call them Frank's Pickles.

2 pounds ripe tomatoes (8 or 9 medium)
2 pounds green tomatoes (8 or 9 medium)
3 large sweet red peppers, seeded
2 large onions
½ cup pickling or kosher salt
2 cups sugar
2 cups cider vinegar
½ teaspoon each mustard seed, ground cloves, and ground cinnamon

Drop the ripe tomatoes into boiling water for one minute, then remove the skins and discard. Chop the ripe tomatoes coarsely. Put the green tomatoes, peppers, and onions through a food chopper, using a medium blade. Combine in a bowl with the ripe tomatoes and add salt, stirring thoroughly. Cover and let stand overnight.

The following day, drain the vegetables, put in a kettle, and add the remaining ingredients. Simmer about one hour, stirring occasionally. Pack into clean, dry, hot half-pint or pint canning jars, filling to within ½ inch of the rims. Seal, and process 5 minutes in a Boiling-Water Bath (page 9). *Yield: 4 to 5 pints.*

Pickled Peaches

3 pounds small, firm, ripe peaches (12 to 15)
Whole cloves (2 for each peach)
3 cups sugar
2 cups cider vinegar
2 cups water
Four 3-inch cinnamon sticks, 12 whole
    cloves, and 1 teaspoon whole allspice,
    tied in a cloth or cheesecloth bag

Dip the peaches in boiling water 10 seconds, then peel away the skins. Stick 2 or 3 whole cloves into each peach. Combine the remaining ingredients in a large kettle and simmer 10 minutes. Add the peaches and continue to simmer until the fruit is just tender, about 15 to 20 minutes.

Using a wooden spoon, pack the peaches into clean, dry pint or quart canning jars. Press down gently, filling to within ½ inch of the rims. Boil syrup, uncovered, until it is slightly thickened, about 10 minutes. Discard the spice bag, and pour the boiling syrup over the peaches, filling to within ¼ inch of the rims. Seal, and process in a Boiling-Water Bath (page 9), 10 minutes for pint jars, 15 minutes for quarts. Let stand at least 2 weeks before using to let the spicy flavor develop. *Yield: 1½ pints.*

Pickled Pears

Substitute juicy ripe pears for the peaches in the recipe for Pickled Peaches (above). Peel the pears (do not dip into boiling water) and proceed with the recipe.

Spicy Pickled Pears

These pickled pears are spicy and great as a garnish for roasted meats, especially game birds. They are best when made with the firm Seckel pears available in the summer. Use fresh gingerroot for this recipe. It is sold in Oriental food shops and by many specialty greengrocers. Leftover gingerroot freezes well, or can be planted in a pot of soil, where the roots will multiply.

2 to 4 firm but ripe pears (about 1½
    pounds)
1½ cups sugar
1 cup water
¾ cup cider vinegar
½ lemon, thinly sliced and seeded
1½ two- to three-inch pieces fresh ginger-
    root
1½ teaspoons whole mixed pickling spices
    and ½ teaspoon whole cloves, tied in a
    cloth or cheesecloth bag

Peel the pears, leaving on the stems; set aside. Combine the remaining ingredients in a medium kettle. Stir over low heat until the sugar dissolves and the mixture reaches a simmer; simmer 5 minutes. Arrange the pears in one layer in the simmering liquid and cook gently until just tender, about 15 to 25 minutes. Using a slotted spoon, remove to a large bowl. (If the pears are too large to be cooked in a single layer repeat the process.) Pour the boiling syrup with all the spices over the pears in the bowl. Cover and allow to stand 12 to 20 hours in a cool place.

Pack the pears into clean, dry quart canning jars to within ½ inch of the rims. Return the syrup and spices to the kettle and heat to a boil. Remove the spice bag and pour the syrup over the pears, filling to within ¼ inch of the rims. Seal, and process 15 minutes in a Boiling-Water Bath (page 9). *Yield: about 2 quarts.*

Watermelon Pickle

You can be very fancy and cut the rind into circles or balls, or be content with cubes.

Rind of ¼ large watermelon (about 2
    pounds rind)
¼ cup pickling or kosher salt
1 quart water
About 18 ice cubes (1 tray)
1 cup water
3 cups sugar
1 cup distilled white vinegar
About 18 to 20 whole cloves and two
    1-inch cinnamon sticks, tied in a cloth or
    cheesecloth bag
½ unpeeled lemon, thinly sliced and
    seeded
Cinnamon sticks

Remove the green skins and all the pink flesh from the watermelon rind. Cut into 1-inch cubes, circles, or balls, and place in a large bowl. Mix the salt with the quart of water and pour over the rind. Add the ice cubes and let stand 5 to 6 hours. Drain, then rinse well in cold water. Place in a kettle with 1 cup of water and boil slowly until just tender, about 30 to 40 minutes (don't overcook). Drain; return to the bowl.

Put the sugar, vinegar, and the spice bag in a small saucepan; boil slowly over medium heat 5 minutes. Pour over the watermelon rind (include the spice bag). Add the lemon slices. Let stand overnight.

The following day, transfer the ingredients to a kettle. Bring to a boil and boil slowly over medium heat until the rind is translucent, about 10 minutes. Pack the hot rind loosely into clean, dry half-pint or pint canning jars, filling to within ½ inch of the rims. Add one whole cinnamon stick to each jar (break sticks in half if half-pint jars are used). Fill the jars with boiling syrup to within ¼ inch of the rims. Seal, and process 5 minutes in a Boiling-Water Bath (page 9). *Yield: 2 pints.*

Cantaloupe or Citron Melon Pickle

Substitute cantaloupe or citron melon rind for the watermelon rind in the recipe for Watermelon Pickle (left).

Pickled Oysters

An amazing number of foods can be pickled deliciously — even oysters. When you've pickled everything else that intrigues you, try these. Use within two weeks for very best flavor.

1 quart shucked oysters, with their liquor
1/3 cup white wine vinegar
½ dried hot red pepper, seeded
1 blade of mace or ⅛ teaspoon ground
    mace
4 whole cloves
1 tablespoon whole allspice

Drain the liquor from the oysters into a saucepan. Bring to a boil and skim the foam. Lower the heat, add the oysters, and poach over very low heat about 3 to 4 minutes. When the oysters are plump and their edges are curled, remove with a slotted spoon and pack into clean, dry pint canning jars, filling to within ½ inch of the rims. Strain the pan juices through a colander lined with cheesecloth, return to the saucepan, and add the remaining ingredients. Simmer the mixture for 15 minutes, then remove from the heat and let cool. Fill the jars with the pickling liquid to within ¼ inch of the rims. Cover with lids and store in the refrigerator. *Yield: about 2 pints.*

Index

B C D E